LLC BEGINNER'S GUIDE FOR ASPIRING ENTREPRENEURS

How to Start a Small Business, Form and Run a Limited Liability Company Dealing with Accounting and any Tax Brake the IRS allows

By

Gregory Olson

TABLE OF CONTENTS

INTRODUCTION 3
CHAPTER ONE 4
  What Is LLC? - All That Needs to Be Known..4
  Is an LLC Right For You? 6
  The Benefits of LLC for Small Business Owners 9
  Using a Demand Letter to Benefit Your LLC...11
  An Explanation of LLCs - The Advantages and Disadvantages.......................12
  LLC Mistakes - How to Avoid Them...13
CHAPTER TWO 17
  The Basics of LLC Formation 17
  Start an LLC, It Is Not Even the Beginning...17
  What Is LLC All About? What You Need To Know 19
  Remarkable Benefits of LLC for Property Owners..20
CHAPTER THREE 22
  LLC: Incorporating Success in Your Business 22
  Choice of Business Entity - S Corporation or LLC?..23
  How to Set Up Your Own LLC 31
  The Rules of a Single Member LLC...32
CHAPTER FOUR..35
  Start Up Choice - Corporation Inc Or LLC? 35
  Elements of an LLC Operating Agreement..37
  LLCs and Liability Protection 41
  LLC Operating Agreement Drafting - Minority Member Tips 43
  Is a Limited Liability Company the Right Entity for Your Business? 46
CHAPTER FIVE..51
  Flexibility and Default Rules 51
  Series LLC - Where Angels Fear to Tread 54
  The Wrong Business Structure Can Destroy Your Financial Future.................57
  Real Estate Tax Strategies and Forming an LLC 59
CHAPTER SIX 66
  Entity Formation Fundamentals...66
  Financial Privacy Using Legal Entities..69
  Common Business Structures 72
  Choosing a Business Entity 77
  Insider Tips to Increase Your Number of Real Estate Investments 83
  Incorporation for Home Based Businesses 87
CONCLUSION 90

INTRODUCTION

The Limited Liability Corporation (LLC) has been an efficient tool for decades to protect your personal assets from the responsibility of apartment rental property. To receive this security shield, however, a business must be carried out in full compliance with the LLC statutes. There are several potential errors that can all be stopped by keeping an experienced LLC lawyer. If the LLC is not properly used, its protections will seriously be jeopardized.

LLC is a key level of asset security with tax benefits that any investor who plans to remain in business and prosper in the long term can introduce. Before you create a home, it is necessary to have a solid foundation to know the laws and IRS rules before you engage in business transactions. The government provides businesses and real estate owners a tremendous benefit when it comes to tax deductions, and the corporation is the key to success.

Want to start your own company today? Well, if your response is YES, you will have to consider the sort of business enterprise you want to set up to meet your business needs. In reality, LLC is one of the most demanded businesses today, which can give you and your company a range of benefits.

CHAPTER ONE
What Is LLC? - All That Needs to Be Known

For a 'limited liability company,' the term 'LLC' is a short form. It is a relationship that makes two forms of partners. In this business management framework, the partners who care for the company or company's affairs are responsible for their debts. However, there are a number of incentives for limited partners and affiliates, such as tax gain and liability insurance.

The Way to Form an LLC

Business individual who want to start a business with LLC (those may be investors or even owners) send the form to the State Secretary. The partners must provide all the essential details and documents before beginning an LLC. You can also file the latest date on which you intend to dissolve the LLC. The number of partners and managers is another significant detail to provide.

Advantages of LLC

No single entity is held responsible for any loss or debt. It is also a risk-free way to invest in companies.

LLC does not limit the arrangement that representatives conclude for their managers and partners. The members are free to enter into contracts and add in them all their obligations and duties.

Members will split their income however they wish. There is no such tax from the corporation.

Instead of the other partners, the partner offers his skills and experience and runs the business; this promotes the work.

The LLC has several other benefits. It is important to remember, however, that this organization's laws vary from country to state.

The LLC is a creature of national legislation. Wyoming was the first country in 1977 to pass a law giving rise to a limited liability corporation. Since that time, all

States in the United States have passed a series of laws that authorize the creation, by statute, of a legal entity called a limited liability corporation.

The LLC came into being large because small company owners wanted a legal body that was more affordable than a corporation that was more appropriate for larger companies.

Lawmakers want to promote small businesses as they drive our economy and build jobs. Consequently, what the LLC provides is a legal body that offers benefits tailor-made for the small business owner, but also has the versatility of accommodating larger corporations.

WHAT CAN A LIMITED LIABILITY COMPANY OFFER TO A SMALL BUSINESS?

The LLC creates a shield for business owners. Owners are not directly responsible for the company's debts and commitments. This kind of legal entity also offers a single taxation layer that minimizes taxes on shareholders and allows active members to deduct from other incomes if the company generates losses.

Security and taxes do not end with income. The limited liability company also provides flexibility for business owners to change how they want to run and manage their business. You don't have to fit into a standard size that fits all governance systems.

Business owners tend to spend time constructing their companies and not holding legal persons or complying with legal enforcement criteria. The LLC legislation was particularly designed to encourage the use of this vehicle. The establishment and management of a limited liability company is a minimum prerequisite.

Another advantage is that a lawyer's use of a corporation transmits a more professional and official profile. Customers understand that the company is a limited liability company and that the company has been seriously designed by its founders. This is nice to do more business.

So, if we ask what LLC stands for, the reply is that it stands for the most common small business legal entity vehicle. A company owner gets immense benefits and advantages for low prices.

Is an LLC Right For You?

State laws vary as they relate to requirements and fees for filing. You must adhere to the laws applicable to the state or states in which you are participating.

LLCs are one of the most commonly used companies. Most of the time, the company owner shapes the company with dire tax implications without consulting an experienced company or a tax consultant. Even the NYS State Division of Companies Website mentions this fact *"Therefore, it is advisable to review, with a close look at the tax consequences, the business situation when deciding which organization to form."*

I emphasized the last sentence because it's the subject of this debate. In fact, a multitude of LLCs has been created for the wrong reasons with catastrophic consequences for companies and their owners who will bear the burden of that decision for years to come and probably for decades to come.

I will discuss what LLC is and why it is unacceptable for most small and micro-businesses that are created. We will also discuss alternatives to using an LLC as a business framework and potential options for established businesses and doing business as an LLC.

Before we know why the LLC system is incorrect for your company, we should look at what it really is, how it came about, and how it operates.

A Limited Liability Company (LLC) is the combination of a company and partnership. LLCs closely mimic and are taxed like partnerships, but they are limited liability benefits like companies.

LLCs are established by registering a unique name through the secretary of state in the state where the company is located. Each state has it the particular rules and fee schedules for forming an LLC. The cost of establishing an LLC in NYS is considerably more costly as a consequence of the need to publish a notice of intent.

AN LLC TAX STATUS

There is a tax status for each legal method of doing business associated with that method, as well as various rules and regulations for each type of company. While the consequences of the legal liability are not the focus of this article, I must mention that to illustrate the reasons why people decide to create an LLC and why it may not be the right option.

The basic forms available to small companies are summarized here.

Incorporated corporation, with one owner, without legal distinction between them and the business, i.e., limitless legal liability. Unincorporated business owners report their returns to Schedule C and are included in their personal tax returns.

Partnership-Another unincorporated partnership and the same unrestricted legal responsibility as a sole proprietor, a partnership has more than one owner (the owner may not have to be an individual, but I'm going to make it simple) and files his tax return on the form 1065. Each partner receives a K1 showing the revenue, expenditures, and other things that the partner declares on his own tax.

C-Corp- a corporate corporation independent of its owners. Owners have restricted legal liability, which means, for the most part, that owners are not at risk of doing business outside their companies. Note that there were always exceptions to this rule, and I do not cover issues of legal liability.

S-Corp – the same as a C-corp, but without the tax features of the corporation. No corporate tax. The shareholder collects K1 from the corporation and reports on his personal tax return revenue, deductions, and other papers.

Now we come to LLC. That's just a limited company. The owner/s enjoy the same limited liability rights as their shareholders. That's great when we get into the tax aspect. You can see that an LLC has no tax classification. The IRS lends to LLC what we call a "default" classification.

Allow me to clarify a couple of tax details. A single-member LLC defaults on the role of the sole proprietor in relation to tax purposes. There are two main drawbacks to this. First, sole proprietors are far more likely to face the IRS audit than a corporate body. Second, profits are subject to social security tax.

The default classification is the partnership, which will file its return on Form 1065. Again, all the earnings are subject to taxes on social security, even though the parties have not earned money. Please note that social security is levied on "active" revenue and does not extend to activities such as land. Again, the partnership does not include the LLC with more than one member.

An LLC is very suitable in some cases, such as when you purchase land. I think the issue is that you want to be an LLC because it sounds great. This is the latest trend. You won't understand tax consequences until late in time. Most of the time, it's an S-corp, which is the most suitable way to work in a small business.

Relief can be sought by means of IRS Form 8832. This form must be filed within 75 days from the date the entity was created, and a possible late election relief occurs if it was not filed in due time.

MICRO BUSINESS SUCCESS CENTERS are the world's leading micro-business success solution. By implementing our ideology and using our services, micro-business owners can be made the presidents of their businesses. Per capital, businesses have become valuable, saleable assets that can sustain their owners.

Pro-Biz Aid Incorporated: helps individuals who are interested in profitability and personal success by providing information, direct guidance, tools, and resources to realize their full potential.

Pro Bookkeepers Inc.: By utilizing existing technology as well as our excellent experience in accounting, office management, schedule management, and customer support, we will work with you in providing you the infrastructure you need to run your company rather than running your business.

Pro Micro Business Marketing: Our marketing specialist team is specialized in marketing for micro-businesses. Conventional marketing and advertisement are not only expensive, but it simply does not meet the needs of the owner of a micro-business.

The Benefits of LLC for Small Business Owners

The Benefits of LLC

It is no secret today that most SMEs prefer an LLC as their business entity. The advantages of LLC are very simple, given that multiple factors are really important in creating a limited liability company: the intermediate cost and effort to continue creating an LLC. But what is the advantage of an LLC for a small company owner?

Minimum expenses, LLC, can be easily shaped private by simply finding and adding your company details with template posts. It really takes about 15 minutes.

LLC Operating Agreement

These businesses are made up of articles. The Company should create an LLC's Operating Agreement to control business activities, whether you intend to have a single or several members. Partnerships frequently fail, and in any disagreement or legal action that arises, this operating arrangement is the definitive and deciding factor. The good thing about an operating agreement as it is also able to avoid legal actions against partners is that, in most situations, the terms of the agreement are explicitly specified in the operating agreement.

Excellent defense of liability. These business organizations can definitely shield a business owner from someone who wants to prosecute him. If you sign properly and work for the organization, you will have no problem in lawsuit and sign as its management member or its member. This is, therefore, so that you do not insert your personal expenses into your company account and are running your bank account as a company. The courts will investigate how you run the company and do it on your own. If the corporation is on its own two feet, has its own accounts and expenses independent from the employees, and if you have not deferred the company reports with the state, you would be well-positioned to protect yourself from liability. This also means that you have not committed fraud; in the event, you are facing a trial, these institutions do not defend against fraud, if the opposing party may demonstrate fraud, it quickly gets into the corporate veil.

LLC Taxation

Certainly, the LLC tax is distinct from corporate tax. The LLC S business policy helps to reduce the self-employment tax or to fully avoid it. You have all the usual business tax write-offs open to you. However, if you work solely under the corporate agency for your company, you cannot escape a tax on self-employment. You can look for an accountant and understand a corporate structure that can mitigate self-employment tax. An example of this is an S Company which pays you to form your limited liability company. There is a lot of LLC information about Internet taxes that you can find. Different tactics shift year by year what appeals most to business owners to the concept of avoiding self-employment tax. Becoming an employee of your own company is the technique that is mostly sought. What's more, your LLC pays for a business. Paying a small income, thus paying large dividends, lowers net tax further. These techniques can be very complicated and require thorough study and good CPA implementation.

Limited Liability Company

In the initial stages of your business, it's all right to just start operating with your LLC and earn more than an accountant. Forming a corporation is usually more costly at the state level and requires more laws and regulations in place to ensure enforcement and corporate custody.

Using a Demand Letter to Benefit Your LLC

Are you familiar with a letter of request, and how your company can benefit? You are very sure that every customer pays every bill on time when you form an LLC. It's not so easy as any of your customers simply would not pay when you form an LLC. But try a letter of the request before you go to court, which will help you obtain the desired outcomes and save money and time. Demand letters help to settle 30 percent of all future conflicts between LLCs and other companies. The beauty of a letter of request is that it is cheap and not difficult, just a simple, succinct letter requesting payment. If the consumer makes no payment or no agreement is reached, you have produced additional paperwork to take before a court.

People do not expect a small company owner to tackle the debt with the same rigor as a big company. Thus, they will sadly neglect your polite attempts to obtain payments. A letter from your LLC is stating why you owe, what you owe, and the legal alternative if you don't pay shows that you are serious and willing to appear before court. Sometimes, the prospect of having to appear before the judge and face their debt publicly is enough to make them pay. You want as much to avoid court as much as you can.

The best way to represent your LLC is through a well-written letter. In order to make the request letter successful, you want to include a few main items:

- A debt history. While the client should know why it owes it and the efforts you have made to recover it, it does provide a comprehensive history for the judge if you have to go to court.
- Enter the unique results you are looking for. For e.g., '$250.00 must be completely paid on or before the 1st of July.'
- Professional look and sound. Your letter of request represents your LLC. Type a letter on the letterhead of the company. Avoid misrepresentation and keep the content company linked. Give a copy to the customer and retain a copy of your documents.

- Conclude your letter by stating explicitly that you intend to take legal action if your request is not fulfilled. For e.g., "If the full amount is not paid before July 1, $250 will be added to the amount immediately."

In an ideal world, you offer a decent product and the customer pays promptly. Before then, consider presenting a request letter and use your precious time to run your LLC.

An Explanation of LLCs - The Advantages and Disadvantages

Limited Liability Companies or LLCs are among their most common company forms for entrepreneurs who start new projects. If you have ever looked at the names of companies selling your products and services, some of them may have corporate names that end in "LLC." Basically, an LLC is a company type. It is one of your choices if you have ever considered starting your own company. But you need to read more about LLCs to see if they are the right kind of company for you before registering your business in this way.

The founders of the LLC, also known as "members," are therefore not directly responsible for the company's debts and costs. You may ask, "But don't other business types, like corporations, have this form of protection?" Yes, other business types may provide limited liability to you, but the LLC has other advantages.

It's pretty quick to shape, first of all. Most states have forms that you can only send in to download. In most countries, the fees that you pay are insignificant (unless you want to process them quickly). In the long term, the records and documents needed by the LLCs are typically also simpler.

Another advantage of an LLC is that you can vote for taxes. You could choose to be taxed as a partnership, S or C. For many business owners, especially those who want to profit from cheaper taxes, this flexibility is attractive.

When you talk about taxes, you don't have to worry about double taxation unless you have decided to get taxed as a C business or have formed your LLC in the district of Columbia. You are charged with the same salary only once. This benefit makes LLC an enticing option for people who run a freelance or consulting enterprise.

Given its benefits, an LLC is also disadvantaged. One big downside is that you cannot sell the company's stocks or shares. This makes expanding a company difficult, especially for companies that expect to be published one day. Furthermore, if one owner wishes to leave the company, LLC must dissolve with the remaining owners and reform them again if they want to continue to operate the company together.

The LLC is also a new agency. As a consequence, it does not have the reputation of faith attached to a company or other form of enterprise. This makes it more difficult to find capital if you are searching for external investors. This also means that national laws on LLCs also vary since there is no particular agreement on how the government can deal with them fiscally and administratively.

As you can see, LLCs have their own perks and drawbacks as any other company structure. It is up to you, the business owner, to decide if the benefits of creating an LLC value the disadvantages you face.

LLC Mistakes - How to Avoid Them

For decades, LLC has been an efficient method to protect your personal assets against the liability of apartment rental property. This defense is extended by the state governments to promote investment, which in turn strengthens the economy and benefits society.

Fortunately, one of the main functions of our company and LLC laws is that private investors should be shielded from personal responsibility in order to support society and the general public. In order to receive the security shield, however, a business must be carried out in full compliance with the LLC statutes. Any of the serious mistakes people frequently make while trying to set up their own LLC or when they enlist support from a discount legal document service, a paralegal, an accountant, or even an attorney not specialized in preparation for

LLC. (Although a tax accountant's services are of considerable value, they are generally not carried out from an asset security point of view).

#1 LLC Mistake. Wait before a tenant claims an injury or has started civil proceedings against you. If the LLC does not exist until a tenant claims or takes legal action, you gain zero insurance for your personal assets if you then make the LLC. It never ceases to confuse me how many consumers panic and try to hurry into the creation of an LLC after they have already been sued. It's always too late at that point.

#2 LLC Mistake. If the rental property is not properly transferred to the LLC when the LLC is formed. An LLC gives its owners asset security only when the underlying rental property is transferred to and retained by the LLC. The use of a Grant Deed or Quitclaim Deed, which must be carefully worded and legally notarized, is a significant move. Unfortunately, there are many individuals who have not done so on their own by using a paralegal or document preparation service. If not done correctly, errors or omissions will lead to an unintentional and needless reassessment of property tax in any detail. A reassessment caused by the customer who previously wanted to move his property without proper instructions can be very costly to reverse. In retrospect, the authors of these errors wished to have hired an accomplished LLC lawyer from the very beginning.

#3 LLC Mistake. If the LLC bank account is not opened and all LLC businesses operate from this account. While some of my new customers have formed an LLC, they have continued all LLC banking transactions through their personal accounts or DBA. All revenue created by the LLC must be put on the LLC account, and all LLC expenses paid out of the LLC account must be paid. If a lawsuit fails to distinguish LLC funds from personal funds, a judge will disallow the LLC, allowing creditors to threaten and seize personal properties. The tenants must make their rental checks payable to the LLC and deposit these checks in the LLC account.

The LLC account must pay for all costs, including but not limited to mortgage payments, insurance, taxes, and maintenance. In an emergency, you can periodically pay an LLC cost by using your personal funds and then write an LLC check to repay yourself. This can, however, be held to an absolute minimum. Furthermore, your LLC should be fitted with a credit/debit card for small property transactions. If you use an agency that collects rental under your name, the agency must transmit rental income to the LLC, not to you directly.

#4 LLC Mistake. Shape a business rather than build an LLC for your rental property. In an effort to save money, however, many individuals mistakenly form a company for their rental property without proper legal guidance. This is a bad idea as a company does not necessarily protect this kind of business as much as an LLC. Corporations often include extra tax filings and formalities, such as required meetings and business minutes. Even if you subsequently want to be taxed as a business, by filing the corresponding forms, you can choose for IRS to treat your LLC as an S or C company.

I have had several clients who paid for their business a paralegal or legal document service in creating an LLC or company. It was only later that they discovered significant issues and, after sought legal aid. Deep dissatisfaction arises as they know that they have paid a lot of money for worthless or wrong papers, as well as franchise taxes, and had to begin from scratch.

#5 LLC Mistake. Don't move your LLC to your Living Trust. If you have a Living Trust, it is necessary to ensure that your LLC becomes your trust or owns it. I encountered several new customers who did not transfer their LLC into their family trust. If they had died before we could settle the issue, the LLC and its assets would be checked and not aimed at the heirs, as the trust is intended to do. This is another field in which adequate legal advice is important to ensure that your properties are not only safe from legal action but also are maintained and safe against the probate and probably excessive property taxes.

Many other errors can be avoided if an experienced LLC lawyer is retained. It is not wise to ensure that your LLC is properly formed and run if you have made the decision to create an LLC. The LLC is a legal instrument. However, failure to use it properly jeopardizes the safeguards it can provide.

CHAPTER TWO
The Basics of LLC Formation

If you choose LLC training for your company, a flexible benefit distribution is an advantage you will have. This is beneficial in LLC training sessions because you can choose how benefits are shared among LLC participants. In a sole proprietorship, all income would obviously be shifted to the sole owner. The benefits are equally distributed between the two partners in a relationship. In an LLC, you can determine how the benefit will be distributed among members based on the amount of capital each participant has contributed.

In most LLC formations, the benefit allocation is divided by the contribution of each member to capital. For instance, if Member A pays $5,000, and Members B and C contribute $20,000 each, then dividing profits would not be fair. In cases like this, members who contributed the greatest proportion of capital should be given the greater percentage of income, Member B and C should get about 45 percent of income in this example, and Member A should get only 10 percent due to the contribution of each member. The thing to keep in mind is that not only money members can contribute cash, working hours, or even equipment.

While the benefit is divided according to the amount of capital each participant contributes in most LLC formations, it does not have to be this way. You may opt to divide the income differently, but you may need to send a few additional papers.

Start an LLC, It Is Not Even the Beginning

Information provided in this book is not legal advice but may contain general legal information without any warranty of any sort. If you have any legal concerns or have a problem requiring legal consultation, please contact an attorney immediately.

An LLC will be created or incorporated at some stage. This occasionally occurs when you start other times after you've run your company for a while. When you start an LLC, some things need to be done to ensure full security for your LLC.

You must hold the training meeting where you actually launch an LCC. This meeting deals with what the LLC is about. During this conference, topics such as LLC ownership, LLC voting rights, and LLC operations should be discussed.

In order to support you at this crucial time when you start an LLC, I highly suggest seeking a lawyer who has expertise in developing LLCs and companies. Each LLC is a special organization that spends a little extra money now and saves you tons of time and money in the future. I can't really emphasize this enough. I think that a fair price to get a lawyer to do all the work to start an LLC or a company is approximately $1,500.00. I've invested nearly $10,000 in starting an LLC. It then became a company that ultimately sold more than $5 million, so the price wasn't so high.

Your LLC operating agreement or corporate regulations provide real power and security. And the correct corporate formalities such as routine board meetings that have been recorded and two of the most commonly ignored corporate formalities have been passed.

So, invest your money and time in getting a solid operating agreement or regulations drawn up by a lawyer before you start an LLC.

I know a lot of people do not have a lot of money for starting an LLC and financing their company and paying for living costs, so they eventually cut corners. One choice is to enter into a more generic LLC operating arrangement or company regulations and to maintain impeccable business records. When you change the LLC operating agreement or corporate regulations, passing resolutions may take place.

When you meet to discuss the establishment of your LLC, you file with the state to start an LLC. If you deal with a lawyer, they generally do it for you. If you work closely with a lawyer and resources, ask if they will draft your LLC operational agreement or corporate agreements and send them to the state. This saves you some money, and you can spend money on a stronger LLC agreement.

When you start an LLC, several things have to be taken into account. Just as I advise my customers to always start with a strong foundation, the stronger the foundation, the easier it will be to do it all. So spend your time and money when you start an LLC to do it all right.

What Is LLC All About? What You Need To Know

Want to start your own company today? Well, if your response is YES, you will have to consider the type of business company you want to set up to meet your business needs. Indeed, LLC is nowadays one of the most demanded enterprises that can give you and your company different advantages. Setting an LLC will allow you to take care of your personal property, lower your tax rate, and even save time by submitting unnecessary formalities. In reality, LLCs grow ideally as they combine a company's limited liability protection and pass-through taxation of companies automatically.

LLC is not a company but rather a structure approved by state officials. This is essentially a distinct form of company that gives other firms and corporations opportunities by combining the corporate benefits with the relationship advantage that transcends taxation. LLCs become increasingly common because it is very practical to use and allows you to avoid deficiencies and problems such as double taxation and needless formalities. Furthermore, they are more versatile and require fewer repetitive formalities than other firms. So if you today want to build your own company without problems, the only thing you can do is to choose the right and trustworthy organization to meet all your needs and to help you when deficiencies occur. Therefore, registering or applying at LLC is easy; all you have to do is visit their website, fill out all relevant details, and wait for your approval.

In addition, LLC owners are often referred to as members as most States do not regulate ownership, so members may include individuals, companies, other LLCs, and even international organizations. In fact, an infinite number of members can exist, but the majority of States allow a single LLC member. If the LLC evolves as a manager, a participant may further remind the shareholders, as they do not take part in the management until their project has improved.

Therefore, if the LLC does not run administrators, participants are explicitly like partners because of their straightforward decision-making.

Remarkable Benefits of LLC for Property Owners

Immobilien has more than ample sources and sites for endless possibilities, particularly for property owners. The most favored and valued means of producing income are rental investments. In recent years, however, most landlords incur significant losses due to lawsuits and complaints brought by tenants and landlords in legal proceedings.

May owners of properties are still figuring out how LLC operates and how it can really bring them the benefits they want. For example, submitting or forming a business organization through LLC means that it has the right to different advantages of joining a company. This involves covering your personal properties from insurance damages and inconsistencies. This is a timely solution for landlords who often suffer more losses from their leasing firms than the extra profits their company plans to receive. LLC does not allow you to risk your personal estate anymore because it is effectively secured and is immune from payment responsibilities resulting from tenant lawsuits and grievances.

However, the difference in entering LLC is that the advantage for single owners is certainly yours, as opposed to becoming a shareholder in a company. In addition, you handle and run your rental company as you wish without intervening with or following the terms and conditions and strict business terms of your co-owners or partners. After all, it is certainly not a piece of cake to organize and to become a part of a group. You should be subject to strict government regulations and laws to authenticate and certify your business company. You need a lawyer, and the fee for a lawyer is certainly a heavy one. The company's license is often very boring, time-consuming, and needs financial allocation.

The tax cuts and benefits reflect another remarkable value and advantage that LLC can offer. For example, one of the main drawbacks of running a business is the double tax that you have to pay. In the LLC, you are not eligible for double taxation because only single owners of a rental company have to pay tax. You are also not only receiving cash because you have all the benefits for ownership alone but are also excluded from the strong obligation to comply with dual taxation.

Paperwork is often imminent and burdensome when it comes to the business. You have to provide and send important documents to create and certify your business. If you just apply for sole ownership, you go to the local construction authority, register the company, apply for an LLC, and continue your company while taking advantage of its rewards.

Real estate owners with rental investments are truly at the forefront of this business type. Forming one protects yourself against imminent losses that you never want to encounter in your house.

CHAPTER THREE
LLC: Incorporating Success in Your Business

By establishing an LLC, the industries from real-estate to construction will reap various benefits and give the company and its customers more opportunities.

LLC is a company structure that enables your company to enjoy legal liability such as that of a company while avoiding annual reports, distributions of shares, regulations, and other requirements when it establishes a company.

Forming an LLC is particularly beneficial for emerging companies. It combines the control and tax benefits of a relationship with minimal transparency. Members of LLC are often shielded from corporate liability or lawsuits. An LLC is more versatile than a company because members may be foreign persons, trusts, associations, businesses, and non-residents. Plus, maintenance is simple; LLC has fewer formalities and is simpler to operate than a company.

Variations in the LLC relative to the business

- Companies are owned by ownership shares or inventories that are distributed to shareholders. Like partnerships, an LLC actually belongs to its members or managers.

- In comparison to LLC, businesses need annual meetings and written minutes. LLC requires less paperwork because these standards do not apply.

- A company has to pay income taxes at the corporate tax rate on its earnings. An LLC is a "pass-through" tax agency, on the other hand. The gains or losses generated by the corporation shall appear on the owners' personal income tax return. Therefore, the double taxation of corporate and personal income tax payable is avoided.

Once you have opted to apply for an LLC, the paperwork will be clarified in two articles with a CD. The Articles of association and the operating agreement are the two articles. They will come along with the corporate or LLC pack.

The Organizational Articles formalize your life according to State law. You have a legal company going after you have filed this.

This document specifies the name, intent, incorporators, quantities, and stock types that may be issued and any other special characteristics of the company. On the other side, the operating agreement includes the LLC's written code of conduct. This requires meetings, board and officer appointments, notices, officer forms and duties, and a standard procedure.

There will also be a registered agent who can accept official documents on your behalf. Examples of documents received are tax advisories, annual reports, and documents relating to the legal process, such as appeals, etc.

The final steps include the submission of an amendment article to reflect the shift of your business from a company to an LLC. You must also submit an original or annual report. Experts in business filing may assist in the processing of required business changes.

Choice of Business Entity - S Corporation or LLC?

LLCs are the most widely used corporations. Since the majority of small and medium-sized enterprises are best organized as either a company or LLC, this article highlights certain fundamental similarities and discrepancies between them. I tried to provide a summary of the following main elements. But note that the following details alone will not allow you to make a proper, informed selection of an individual. This can all be done with the lawyer and accountant's organized support.

C Corporation

The largest firms are C firms. C companies are all publicly traded companies. The term "C" is taken from the Internal Revenue Code, Subchapter C, which controls corporate taxes. There are a number of reasons why C businesses are more appropriate for large firms. Multiple stock groups, infinite number and shareholder forms, a fiscal year versus a calendar tax year, and corporate profit retention are just some of the major differences of a C company. This is generally ideal for companies that want publicly to raise capital or whose class of investors differs.

Most notably, double taxation extends to C companies. This means that all of the profits of the C-company is once taxed at the corporate level, and then the same income is taxed again at the shareholder level when the benefit is a dividend. Double taxation can sometimes be avoided in smaller C companies by annually abolishing net profits by paying to shareholder workers. Shareholders must declare on their personal tax returns any dividend earnings as capital gains.

A business begins as a C business for tax purposes. Unless the shareholder elects "S," corporate tax status as discussed below, all companies will be known as C corporations automatically. The corporation's net profits (after deductions for pay, company expenses, and the depreciation of furniture and equipment) is net. The C business will only be taxed on "effectively related" revenue from a 15% corporate tax rate of the first $50,000 of corporate taxable income per year.

When the organization is listed as a "Personal Service Business" (PSC), a flat fee of 35 percent from the dollar of a net profit would be charged. This is a typically unwanted form of entity. The CSPs are companies whose owners operate in the fields of accounting, acting, architectural, technological, health and veterinary services, law, and performance services. The lowest tax rate of 15 percent is only possible for a business that offers personal services if a person who is not employed by the company holds at least 6 percent of its issued stock. Otherwise, the highest personal tax rate will apply to personal service taxable income in that business. A PSC is, by definition, a C organization. A timely S-election, as discussed below, will therefore negate your company's classification as a PSC and escape the 35% flat tax rate.

Some unique tax benefits are gained by the use of the C Company. The ability to deduct all premiums paid on health insurance for employed owners and their spouses and dependents is one of the main benefits for SMEs. Furthermore, a C company may, at any point during a financial year, enact a MERP (medical, dental, and drug expenses refund plan), which can be easily applied back to the start of the fiscal year and can buy disability insurance for one or more of its managers or other workers. An organization can also exclude disability insurance premiums without the executive or employee's taxable expenses. Finally, an employer will deduct contributions to eligible pension programs.

In terms of ownership, the company is held by shareholders under the ownership of stock (or shares) in the company. Corporations issue their shareholders' stock certificates to show their ownership percentage. C Companies can have different asset groups, such as common and preferred stocks, offering different dividends and voting rights to shareholders. Without affecting the company, shares can be freely exchanged or redeemed. According to Illinois law, like every other Jurisdiction, corporate shareholders typically have a full liability shield from the actions or omissions of the company. The shareholders elect a board of directors who then oversee the company's operations and businesses. The law of Illinois requires the appointment of President, Secretary, and Treasurer, while sole shareholder companies are allowed.

The corporation's Bylaws are its guiding text. The bylaws regulate the business and affairs of the company (C and S companies) and define the amounts, powers, and obligations of the board of directors, the voting rights of the shareholder, the dissolution of the company, annual meetings, and special meetings and other corporation rules. In general, a stock buying or stock restraint contract or similar agreement regulates the relationship between the owners (shareholders) of a small or closely held company. This instrument can provide for buying and selling rights of shareholders, restrictions on the sale or transfer of shares, and purchase rights for companies, among other items. Corporations shall have a collection of bylaws regulating the company in all jurisdictions, or the corporation shall be subject to the default rules set out in the State statute.

Notice that the arrangement between the corporate owners (shareholders) may also be subject to a separate instrument, such as an inventory purchase or an agreement on the restriction of inventory, shareholder agreement, or similar document. In general, this document governs the transfer and acquisition of stocks, companies, and/or shareholders.

C Corporation is ideally suited to active companies with a chance of appreciating and high share potential. C businesses typically keep their profits in the early stages of growth and do not share corporate income with shareholders to enjoy it.

S corporation
S corporation is a company, much like a C company. Its owners are similarly shielded from personal responsibility for the actions or omissions of the companies.

The key difference lies in the S corporation's tax treatment. As suggested, C companies are taxable at the corporate level, and shareholders are taxed from the same revenue stream as paid as dividends. S companies, by comparison, prevent dual taxation since only individual owners are taxed. The status of a company is achieved by electing such organizational tax treatment (IRS Form 2553). Net profit, including wages paid to workers and shareholder-employees, after expenses incurred for S companies is declared in federal Form 1120S and transferred to shareholders' personal tax return through Schedule K-1, where the return is subject to the regular tax. In addition, pass-through losses are restricted to the basis of the taxpayer in the S company stock.

All salaries are taxed on self-employment (payroll). S Companies shall pay shareholder-employee fair wages in exchange for the services the employee gives to the company before non-wage distribution to the shareholder-employee can be made. The S Company pays the employer's share of FICA tax (7.65%), and the employee pays the balance of the FICA tax (7.65%). For the S company and the shareholder, salaries are subject to a cumulative payroll tax of approximately 15.3 percent plus the shareholder's income tax rate. So, all things considered, the shareholder-employee can only pay a minimum wage to himself in order to minimize taxes on the profit stream of businesses. IRS regulations specify that the shareholder-employee be paid fair compensation (many consider this failure to cause an internal audit). However, any other income avoids self-employment taxation and is either subject to ordinary income or capital gains. This means that payroll taxes can only be levied on fair salaries of employee-holders, not the distributions of the S business.

When do you have to pay salaries? According to the IRS, the shareholder-employee shall assess fair compensation for the S company. The IRS shall investigate the source of the gross receipts of the S company: (1) shareholder services, (2) non-shareholder staff services, or (3) capital and equipment. If the gross receipts and income are obtained from things 2 and 3, the shareholder-employee shall be paid no compensation. However, if the bulk of gross sales and income are related to the personal services of the shareholder, part of the allocation of profit should be distributed as compensation. (Of course, you can seek more information from an accountant).

Even if profits are not allocated to the owners and left as working capital, the individual owners still can be charged. This is because all revenue is directly distributed to shareholders. C-corporate owners are responsible only for dividend taxes they currently collect (although the corporation's undistributed revenue is not subject to the tax of self-employment).

Any drawbacks of the position of the S elections are that the S company holders on whom they pay the deductions on life benefits, disability insurance, car and life, drug, and dental insurance plans will be taxable.

S companies are less versatile than C corporations and LLCs, amongst other main differences. Only a small number of shareholders are permitted, usually individuals and no foreign shareholders. In that context, small and close-owned companies that do not aim to raise significant sums of capital publicly are generally better suited. As for a C venture, the shareholders own the company under their shares in the company. However, unlike a C company, there can only be one type of stock with regards to distribution rights.

Corporations typically have low debt, low risk, and a low chance of major appreciation for active companies as all corporate profits normally are allocated to shareholders.

Limited Liability Company (LLC)

An LLC provides to each of its shareholders the same personal liability shield that a company offers. However, it offers great flexibility in dealing with capital contributions and allocating gains and losses to shareholders. In particular, an LLC will allocate income as it sees fit for its members. For example, assume that you and your partner have an LLC to which you contributed $80,000 of capital and only $20,000 from your partner. If your partner works 80%, the owners will still decide to share the 50/50 profits. However, if you and your partner were shareholders in an S firm, you would have to allocate 80% and 20% to your partner under the statute. If you have any partners, this can be an unfair way to organize your company.

The LLC is taxed as a partnership, as gains and expenses are passed on to the members, and no income tax is charged at the corporate level. The LLC prohibits double taxation, much as the S business does. (Again, some states levy LLC's income substitution taxes). The income of the LLC is shown in Form 1065, then distributed via Schedule K-1 to the owners. The owners then record their personal income (1040) on Schedule E. If the LLC has only one owner, then the IRS considers the LLC automatically as a single owner ("unregarded entity"). A neglected individual does not file a tax return, and the owner declares the profits in compliance with Schedule C of its own return. The IRS will immediately handle the LLC as though it were a partnership if the LLC has multiple owners. However, an LLC is a 'check the box' company, which means that it may choose to be taxed as a corporation.

There is a lot of misunderstanding in terms of self-employment taxes when it comes to LLC members. The disparity in your treatment as a general partner and a limited partner, in general, is important in the calculation of self-employment tax liability since an LLC is taxed as a partnership. If a member of an LLC is regarded as a limited partner, the member's share of LLC profits does not have a self-employment tax (except for all guaranteed payments). If a Member is a general partner, he or she must pay tax on all LLC incomes for self-employment. However, under Section 1.1402(a)-2 of 1997 Proposed IRS Treasury Regulations, if an LLC member has the authority, or provides more than 500 hours per year of service to an LLC, of being directly liable for any debt, that member shall, as the general partner, be taxed and shall have a self-employment tax duty on his LLC revenue allocation. Otherwise, the member will be charged as a limited partner and does not have tax responsibilities relating to its LLC revenue allocations for self-employment.

The LLC may also have two interest groups, one of which shall be treated as a general partnership interest and another which shall be treated as a limited partner interest. If a spouse or member holds both class interests, the member may divide the income share between the two classes, pay self-employment taxes on the general partner side, but not on the restricted partner side. The draft Regulations for 1997 were never formally enforced by the IRS, but many practitioners and taxpayers relied on them. In addition, IRS officials have now confirmed that they can count on it.

Both benefits and losses allocated to members and "salaries" (usually guaranteed payments) paid to them shall be called independent jobs and shall be subject to self-employment taxes. LLC owners are deemed to be self-employed and must pay a 15.3 percent self-employment fee. Note in an S company that only wages are subject to job taxes and not distributions to shareholder workers. The S company thus gives its shareholders substantial job tax benefits as compared to the LLC.

In most cases, LLCs offer limited liability insurance if correctly formed and maintained, but typically there are little to no tax advantages versus sole proprietorship to the corporate partnership. The right of members to restrict the transfer of a membership interest only to the transfer of economic interest is a major advantage of LLC over companies. This means that prospective members will only collect dividends (and pay taxes) but without voting or management rights. If a business shareholder transfers its stock, all ownership attributes, including voting rights, shall follow the move, except where the stock is non-voting stock.

The owners of LLCs are called shareholders, and each member has an interest in the business as a percentage of LLC. LLCs can establish different groups of membership interests similar to C corporations. Members include companies and other LLCs, which provide this organization with ultimate flexibility in its ownership structure. An LLC is typically operated by its members, where the LLC's company and operations are operated by its members themselves, or where either a Member Manager or a foreign manager is named. LLCs are commonly controlled by members. Illinois provides one-member LLCs, like most other nations, if not all. Unlike several other jurisdictions, Illinois also requires licensed service providers, such as lawyers and physicians, to create LLCs for business operations.

The Operating Agreement is the LLC's guiding text. It is identical to corporate regulation, which effectively regulates the same aspects. Most jurisdictions, however, state the contents required in bylaws and operating agreements and, of course, there are different requirements. The relationship between the members of an LLC is often set out in the operating agreement, while for some rights of shareholders, companies usually use different instruments, such as stock transfer and buy-out rights of companies.

Real estate investments and companies holding other properties that typically expose their owners to liability risks are generally suitable for LLCs. Obviously, if you have one or more partners and want flexibility in how the organization distributes benefits (and losses) to its members, then the LLC is likely to be the right option.

How to Set Up Your Own LLC

A limited liability corporation, or LLC, is a legal organization in the United States that provides many benefits to business owners. An LLC offers the owner of the company a limited liability as well as some different tax advantages. You may choose to set up an LLC with an attorney, use it, or do it yourself online. The LLC setup can be a great way for simple business startups with only one owner and a simple business model themselves.

Why Choose an LLC?

Liability and taxes are some of the main concerns when beginning a new business entity. Different corporate structures include LLC, limited company (LP), alliance, C- and S-Corporation and sole ownership. There are also other, less popular variants. All these organizations impact the owners' liability. An LLC restricts the responsibility of business owners to the value of their investment. They are not responsible for this waste. The second major factor in the creation of an organization is taxation. In a limited liability company, the shareholders can opt to be taxed either as a company or as a passing party. This gives the business a great deal of versatility.

LLC Tax Advantages

The principal tax gain of a limited liability firm is the opportunity to be treated either as a corporation or as a pass-through organization. As a pass-through company, the revenue and expenses are allocated to the owners through their personal tax returns. Double taxation can also be avoided if an individual is taxed as a corporation.

LLC Formation

You can create an LLC by sending the necessary paperwork to your state. Only find the Secretary of State's website in your state. You have to pay a fee and complete some basic papers. Most states allow the paperwork to be done online. You will have to create organizational articles to justify your limited liability company. If your company is straightforward and you don't have several owners, all this will make sense on your own. Naturally, the services of an attorney may be worthwhile if you have a more difficult case. Make sure you read your LLC application all of the fine print. There are different laws that require you to hold annual meetings and pay some charges to the state to retain your business.

The Rules of a Single Member LLC

As an appealing type of association, the Limited Liability Corporation may be a confusing business structure. In reality, a few significant differences distinguish the LLC from the normal (or limited liability) format.

By definition, the distinction between individual LLC members and ordinary LLCs is that the former has only one member, owner, or manager. The technological gap ends here, but from this status, there are a few other variations.

Note: not all states will always allow you to join a single LLC member, which is a sole proprietorship that you organize instead. This is regrettable because it reduces limited liability rights. However, it is a factor. The good news is that you do not have to live in a state to organize your company (you just want to do business there), so your geographical position does not restrict you. For example, you might live in Nevada and organize an LLC in Delaware, like the way the company operates.

A Risky Endeavor

Unfortunately, because of the existence of LLCs (i.e., partnerships), some of the advantages of LLCs are not usually achieved by their individual members. Many legal professionals would allow you to establish a relationship with your organization, even though you give just two percent of your business to a close family member or friend. This is because of a few complicated rules and laws:

Charge Order Protection

The government forbids your personal creditors from taking properties that belong to the corporation in order to protect them. Rather, you can demand only your personal share of the income created by the company. You render this complex by building an SMLLC. Therefore, you can fill out IRS Form 8832 and opt to have your company taxed as a company to help avoid this.

Death and Operating Agreements

As a sole member of LLC, the organization has a range of limitations (in part because this type of business has emerged as an alternative to a partnership). A major but overlooked benefit for businesses is that they are indefinite – their lives are not related to the lives or well-being of a single person. When an owner (stockholder) dies, the company simply redistributes its ownership and continues. Multi-partner LLCs operate in much the same way as normal. However, single LLCs do not. In this situation, it is necessary to specify in the operating contract who will take over ownership at the death of the owner. This should usually also be supported in the individual's will.

Tax Time

Single LLCs also have unique rules on taxes. The IRS considers the arrangement to be an unrecognized entity and taxes LLCs with one owner in the same manner as it charges sole property.

As always, keep notes and keep your personal finances and company finances apart. This is common for all organizations, but it is particularly important to shape and function an LLC as a single member of convoluted situations.

Although many do not suggest to operate as a single LLC member, the option of other types of activity is possible and potentially better. Always note the complicated state of affairs as you work and keep records and brace yourself (or the will) for a headache.

CHAPTER FOUR

Start Up Choice - Corporation Inc Or LLC?

Many start-up companies are met with the company vs. LLC decision in the early morning. Who's a great choice? Which one offers better defense and tax benefits? Nobody really has an easy and straightforward solution. It depends on the corporation, the ownership structure, the priorities, the priorities, and the state enterprise.

Disclaimer: I am not a lawyer, and the following details should not be treated as legal advice. I highly recommend that you seek legal advice from your lawyer if you want to start a business.

Usually, three categories of organizations are considered by most start-up companies:

- Limited Liability Company (LLC)
- S Corporation (Inc)
- C Corporation (Inc)

Each such organization has its own advantages. Let's start with LLC.

LLC owner's versatility and ease of service in ownership. The ownership of an LLC is not limited. An LLC can be managed by the members of the LLC (the operating agreement specifies how it is managed), which means that the owners manage the business or that the business is managed by an elected manager. An LLC is easier to run because it does not have to comply with the formalities. LLC may also be a "pass-through" company for tax purposes like S Corporation. Profits will be distributed to the owners and recorded in personal income tax records of the owner, thus removing the double taxes normally incurred by the owners of C Company.

On April 15th, LLC owners pay their self-employment tax once a year when income taxes are usually due. Revenue tax returns for LLC owners are also relatively simple. A single LLC member files as sole proprietor the same 1040 tax return, and Schedule C. LLC partners file the same 1065 partnership tax return as owners of conventional partnerships.

Partnership tax return.

For several start-ups, LLC can be the ideal framework. One of the downsides of an LLC is that it doesn't really allow shareholders, so if you want to gain external investors like angel investors or venture capitalists, an LLC probably won't work for you. Some risk capital companies have mechanisms that do not allow them to invest in an LLC, as they have limits on the type of stock that they may issue.

S Corporation has some limits as only 75 shareholders may be within an S company. No non-resident aliens can be shareholders, and no other LLCs or companies can be shareholders.

An S Corporation wants a lot more paperwork than an LLC. It functions like a typical C company, so the same formalities and recording protocols have to be followed. On the other hand, an S Company retains the LLC's tax advantages. The managers or officers of S Corporation manage the business. S Company also has little flexibility in dividing income between its shareholders. The profits have to be allocated according to the share ownership ratio, even though the owners feel different.

One of the biggest distinctions between the S Company and LLC is the income tax. The LLC owner is considered self-employed and, as such, must pay a 15.3 percent self-employment tax to Medicare and Social Security. In LLC, the company's net revenue is taxed on self-employment.

Only the wage paid to the owner/employee is subject to employment tax in an S Company. The remainder of the income paid as a distribution under IRS laws is not subject to job tax. S Company, therefore, has the ability to save on job tax. The downside is extra paperwork in conjunction with a payroll tax. The payroll tax is a charge when you go tax that must be charged annually to the IRS all year round. Tax returns are due on time, or businesses can be subject to fines and interest.

A C Corporation is your typical business, one of the Fortune 500 companies. It is a legitimate tax entity, so you are covered as far as possible but not tax advantages. C Companies should be incorporated in Delaware or Nevada because both countries have a broad legal context for companies, their boards, and their shareholders. One of the problems of C Companies is the need for the board of directors to comply with certain reporting standards very closely and to keep the activities and finances in the general order. C Company can issue to everybody various kinds of stocks (common or preferred). The C Company may have an infinite number of shareholders, and for most venture investors and risk capitalists, this form of company is known and intended. Unfortunately, with a C Corporation, you are going to have double taxation, but most likely, you need to be a C Corporation if you want investors to invest in your company.

One thing to remember is that you can change the form of an entity from one to the other at any point. You just have to weigh the costs of the transition.

Elements of an LLC Operating Agreement

This section discusses the key to intermediate level concerns that should be resolved in operating agreements with two or more members of an LLC. The founding document of an LLC is the organizational papers filed with the LLC chartering State. Most US countries are not required to list all LLC members under their articles of organization and, even if required, their identity will change over time. Thus, LLC's most basic role is to describe the member(s) to third parties who deal with the LLC. Have individual LLC members written operating agreements? Yes, specifically because of the aforementioned explanation (i.e., checking the identity of the member(s) for third parties). The following are the key problems I propose for an LLC operating agreement to resolve.

- Identify the members;
- List initial capital contributions of members (if any);
- List member ownership interests;
- State the method by which member voting shall occur;
- State the method by which profits and losses shall be allocated to the members; and

- If the LLC has managers (as opposed to being managed by all members), identify the manager and state those issues reserved for vote by all members together with a mechanism for the members to remove the manager.

Some of the above are self-explaining, while others need clarification. Where a Member contributes property other than cash as part of the initial capital contribution to the LLC, the contribution of the LLC is based on the contributed assets on the same basis as each contributing member in the assets before the contribution under Section 723 of the Internal Revenue Code. This means that the value allocated to the contributed assets of the LLC books (and also included in the LLC operating agreement as to the initial contributing capital) is dependent on the assets allocated to the contributing member. The costs charged for the asset are usually based on less any provisional depreciation. For more information on the subject, please consult with a tax professional. The ownership interests are usually represented as either unit (accounting to share in a company) or as percentages of the total under LLC's operating agreements. If you delegate percentage interests to the members, make sure that the percentage interests of the members are 100%.

The two primary forms of voting by LLC members are by capital and by equity interest. If an operating agreement stipulates that voting is carried out by capital, each member's vote shall be of equal weight. Members voting on the basis of ownership interest means that each member's vote will be weighed against its ownership interest in the LLC. For e.g., assume XYZ, LLC has three members whose operating agreement states that the members must vote on an equity interest and that their ownership interest is as follows: x-15 percent, Member Y — percent 30, and Member Z-55 percent. In this case, X has had 15 votes, Y 30, and Z 55 of a total of 100 votes cast. If XYZ's operating agreement includes a simple majority, Z will then enact any measure by 55 votes, even though both X and Y are voting against that measure.

The articles of the LLC identify the LLC as managed by all members or managed by managers designed by the members. In order to make it more confusing, called managers may be members themselves. Why does an LLC nominate managers? This occurs more frequently when not all the participants participate actively in the LLC. It can also happen when the LLC majority-owned member(s) are able to conclude an agreement from the minority member(s) that the majority will continue controlling the LLC, excluding the minority. The practicality of making all the members handle the LLC decreases as the number of members increases. In the case of an LLC operated by administrators, very few problems are left for members to determine. The acceptance of new members and the voluntary disbandment of the LLC are two examples. However, members may enter additional constraints into their organizational agreement on the power of LLC managers. For example, credit purchases in excess of a certain dollar sum, the execution of any property lease, salary fixing for employees, etc.

The following is a list of additional problems that an LLC may wish to include in its operating agreement. In an operating agreement, several concerns outside these may theoretically be resolved.

- Required services to be provided to the LLC by any member;
- Mandated cash distributions to members;
- Penalties for failure of member to provide initial capital or agreed services;
- Any matter requiring supermajority vote of members for passage;
- May the LLC require capital contributions from members after formation of LLC?
- Removal of members;
- Withdrawal of members;
- Limits upon the sale or other transfer of membership interests;
- Fiduciary duties members owe to one another; and
- Whether any members shall receive a salary in exchange for services rendered to the LLC.

Small companies frequently find themselves structured as LLCs, where the members earn their membership interest in LLC instead of the donation of money (or the mixture of cash and promised future services in return for promised future services). In such situations, it is important that the LLC operating agreement sets out the services that each member promises to provide to the LLC as comprehensive as possible. In addition, what are the penalties if these facilities are not provided? When the LLC fails, members often switch to other business opportunities leaving the other members to carry out their business. Planning made in advance to deal with this problem will save the LLC members major headaches if the LLC is facing this situation. Themes Members may want to require an overwhelming majority for transit involve entry of new members, decision to dramatically sell all LLC assets, and removal of the manager (if any).

LLC members who are not versed in the LLC's tax burden are always surprised to hear about all the LLC's earnings, regardless of whether the LLC directly distributes cash to them or not. The disgraceful LLC member will incur a tax bill that the LLC does not allocate to cover. This could be particularly burdensome for minority members who lack the power to demand that LLC cash be charged to cover LLC's personal tax liability. This problem can be overcome by requiring that a certain share of the annual income (such as 40 percent) be at least allocated to the participants of the operating agreement each year, where the LLC has a profit. As the amount of benefit allocated to each member remains uncertain until the LLC tax return is finalized, a certain number of days after the LLC tax return is finalized (i.e., 30 days) are typical to the required tax distribution period of the member.

LLC members' removal is a sticky topic. In certain nations, such as Texas, Members have no right, unless the right is given in the LLC Operating Agreement, to withdraw from an LLC (see Texas Business Organizations Code Sec. 101.107). In certain ways, it is like a marriage that members come together to run a small business. Can we not expect divorces? All parties are better off if the participants have in their LLC operating agreement a certain level of intention to withdraw from their participants. Another problem often ignored in the drafting of the operating agreement is fiduciary obligations owed by members. It is especially relevant in this field that members are permitted to carry out business activities outside the LLC and, in particular, if members are permitted to engage in the same business sector as the LLC, which may compete with the LLC. State LLC acts are not unusual to be silent or ambiguous on the subject. For example, Delaware's Limited Liability Company Act fails to note that members or administrators of LLCs who leave the matter to contractual agreements between the parties are performing fiduciary duties.

LLCs and Liability Protection

An inexpensive and very efficient way to secure your properties from attack is to move your property to a limited liability company (LLC). The investment property title owned by an LLC limits its liability only to certain assets held within the LLC. Like shareholders in a company, a properly organized LLC guards its owners against lawsuit liability, including liability for actions of employees and agents.

California LLC will provide you or your investors with some significant benefits. The LLC provides a risk barrier that promotes land ownership and protects the personal property of the owner from litigation and seizures. The double taxation of conventional businesses and lengthy formalities are abolished. Where legal action is required against a resident, such as an eviction, the claim is sought by the LLC rather than the individual owner. Furthermore, the privacy of the owner is improved by paying rental checks to the LLC, by leasing arrangements between the LLC and the tenant, by communication with the LLC.

While high limit liability insurance is essential, the security of the property owner(s) against loss of assets is still not adequate. In several of these policies, mold plumbed paint and other environmental hazards are exempt. In addition, decisions resulting from unfair arguments are rarely protected. Even with high-cost insurance coverage, an event like a fire or a fall on the balcony that could lead to multiple lawsuits could generate responsibility that goes well beyond the policy cap. Also, with the tenants' best intentions, the LLC has become a crucial weapon to restrict liability not just for legal claims but only for claims in which a brainwashed jury can see the validity of this. In comparison with the tremendous value offered, the deductible $800 annual State franchise tax on LLCs is tiny.

The state of Nevada LLC has been replaced by the California LLC in recent years because annual taxes are comparatively small compared with California. However, in most situations, the creation of a Nevada LLC for your California property would have little to no financial gain because possession of the California property inherently implies a company in California. As such, Nevada LLC is also expected to register with the California Secretary of State and to pay California's initial registration fee and $800 annual franchise tax along with the income tax. (See Rev. and Tax Code Sec. 17941, Ca. Corp., Sec. 17050). Nevada LLC / Corporation can be an enticing choice for investors in business projects other than California real estate, where the principal business is not traded in California.

Additional advantages of LLC include LLC's right to use 1031 exchanges and the 3 1/3 withholding allowance for the selling of immovables for multi-member LLCs. Moreover, for single-member LLCs like those held by a husband-wife or living trust, a separate federal tax return is typically not necessary, and the property transfer into the LLC is almost always excluded from tax revaluation. And the LLC is working very well with a living trust to secure and maintain property assets simultaneously.

Many apartment owners have made a living trust in order to distribute their properties when they die, avoid large probation expenses, minimize or cancel estate taxes when they die, and avoid court checks on their properties if they become disabled. However, the living trust would not defend against legal proceedings. If a flat is owned by a living trust directly, then all other trust assets may be subject to legal liability resulting from the building. A much safer solution is to put your apartment in an LLC and create a responsibility buffer to cover all other trust properties. The desires of the LLC members can then be safely applied to the trust.

With respect to multiple investments, it is best for each property to have a separate LLC such that liability from one property cannot be added to any other property. And one-family homes with tenants must be owned by their own LLC. If it is not a feasible choice to pay $800 per annum for several LLCs, properties can be grouped together. The ownership of six investment properties with three in one LLC and three in the other will provide considerably more security than all the properties owned by one person. The use of limited partnerships should consider investors who want to move several properties with annual gross rental receipts totaling more than $500,000 to one company. Both the limited partnership and the LLC must pay the $800 franchise fee, but if the total annual receipts surpass the $250,000, the LLC must then pay the extra gross receipts fee.

Because landlords are subjected to nearly unlimited exposure to their legal proceedings and financial liabilities resulting from ownership of their rental property, they must use any legitimate means to protect their properties. Once a qualified lawyer has prepared and submitted the collection of legal documents needed for the initial creation of the LLC, personal assets are no longer available to meet any obligations or decisions against the LLC.

LLC Operating Agreement Drafting - Minority Member Tips

LLCs are state-owned hybrid corporate organizations. In the case of companies, ownership and management are organized into three levels-shareholders (owners), the board of directors, and officers. LLCs have only one layer most tightly kept. All positions for LLC members are equivalent to shareholders, administrators, and officers. The LLC structure appears simpler on the surface, but it's tricky. The LLC law in most states is very ambiguous in terms of the privileges and obligations of LLC members to each other. The Laws give LLC members a broad range of freedom to establish their LLC operating agreement to govern how the organization functions in operation and address the aggravated members who are affected by the violation of the business agreement.

Required Capital Contributions

In certain countries, a Member's commitment to making capital contributions to the LLC shall not be enforceable unless the Member against whom the compliance is sought has made a promise in writing (usually the Operating Agreement). Find out Florida State. Section 608.4211(2) and Section 17200 of the California Corporate Code. Each operating agreement should specify the amount of capital each participant shall make to the LLC when the contributions are made and in what forms (i.e., cash or other property) the contributions shall be made. When a member contributes property instead of cash, add to the operating agreement a list of the property to be donated, and its agreed value. What if a member does not make capital contributions in compliance with the LLC operating agreement? A quick and efficient reminder is to minimize the ownership interest of the offending participant of the LLC of proportion to its not made capital investment. I am aware, however, that LLC members are unable to arbitrarily decrease the Member's ownership percentage for failure to make the capital contributions necessary unless this solution is contained in the operating agreement.

The secondary capital investments that are needed when the LLC starts operations is another secret problem that returns to bite minority LLC members. Let's assume that in the early years, your LLC loses money and generates the need for additional resources. Minority shareholders should carefully read the terms of the agreement as to which minority members are obliged; otherwise, when a capital call comes from the majority member, it could come as a nasty surprise. If secondary capital calls require unanimous consent from all members, minority members are shielded from unintended capital calls.

Distributions of Capital

For federal tax purposes, LLCs are flow-through corporations. That means that any LLC income is distributed to the members on an annual basis irrespective of whether members currently earn equivalent capital distributions from LLC. Some LLC minority members find it a shock to be taxable on LLC revenue distributions if the LLC wishes to maintain resources and not allocate any or a portion of the revenue to members. One way to protect LLC minority members is to require that a certain proportion of allocated income is distributed not less than a year to LLC members until all members agree otherwise unanimously. 40% is a secure percentage that guarantees that each Member obtains a distribution from LLC sufficient to meet the LLC income allocation's tax liability. For example, suppose that LLC X has $200,000 in income in 2010 with Member 1 with 20 percent ownership interest assigned $40,000 ($200,000 x 20 percent) in income from LLC for that year. If the LLC Operating Agreement stipulates that members must receive a 40% annual income distribution allocation, then Member 1 will receive the necessary capital distribution check of at least $16,000 ($40,000 x 40 percent) from the LLC. This protects minority LLC members from incurring tax liability for which the LLC does not allocate money.

Penalties for Member Failure to Provide Promised Services

LLC participants are usually granted sweat equity, i.e., ownership interest in exchange for their service pledge. Both LLC members' commitments to provide services should be recorded in the business agreement. It is exceedingly difficult to execute oral agreements of this nature unless reported in the operating agreement. The agreement also involves an integration clause, which stipulates that all commitments or agreements between the parties not recorded in the contract are void. Promise recording is just half the war. What is the punishment for not performing the promised services of a member? I am often asked by LLC members if they can kick out a non-performing LLC member and take over the business. The response is 'no' unless your operating agreement clearly reminds you of that. If the arrangement is silent on the seizure of the LLC member's share interest for failure to provide service and aggravated, members may be reminded of a suit for damages by the non-performing LLC member. Litigation is an expense and a long way to claim compensation.

Member Right of Disassociation

As a minority member, oversight of the LLC's activities is typically kept by the majority. What if you disagree with the LLC's organizational or strategic direction after operations start? In most states, an LLC member does not withdraw unless the LLC operating agreement stipulates this right. A minority member can be caught in an LLC like a bad marriage. It is useful to secure a right of withdrawal from LLC operations, but the conditions on which withdrawal is permitted are also of great practical importance. If an LLC member has a large capital account at the time of withdrawal, how much, when, and when the LLC paid the capital account is an important aspect of the Operating Agreement.

Is a Limited Liability Company the Right Entity for Your Business?

Should you run your business as a corporation? Or is there a different, easier alternative?

You probably also noted that in the last 10 years there have been more and more companies with their names preceded by the letters "LLC" rather than "Inc." "LLC" refers to a limited liability company, is the newest form of legal entity in the USA and is the perfect union, for many entrepreneurs, between the tax benefits of a limited partnership and the limited liability characteristic of a company. Now available in all 50 countries, including non-US countries.

Limited liability corporations are the newest child on the block in the United States when it comes to legal organizations doing business. In 1977, the state of Wyoming passed legislation to create this new body for the first time. By 1999 all fifty States had introduced legislation in the United States to allow this exciting new legal entity to be established.

But why is the LLC so appealing to lawmakers? And why did so many entrepreneurs settle on the LLC rather than a "C" company or even an "S" company? Most importantly, how do you determine if it's right for you?

Maybe the most significant explanation is that the LLC serves the needs of both accountants and lawyers. Accountants tend to favor the Limited Partnership as they worry about the risks of 'double taxation' when their customers use a company: when their company receives dividends, the company pays its income tax, and the shareholders pay the same benefit tax again when they are levied on the dividends earned. In comparison, lawyers typically prefer the higher asset security provided by the company's limited liability to all its shareholders.

The LLC is a limited company (and an S-corporation) because the LLC's share of the net profits or losses for the year "passes on" to the income taxpayer's 1040 individual tax return. It is a pass-through organization. The LLC itself is subject to no separate levy. On the other hand, the LLC is just like a business, because unlike the limited partnership, requiring an ultimate partner responsible for all the consequences of the partners' decisions and actions, all its members enjoy limited liability.

People choose to form LLCs primarily because they choose to set up an S-corporation or limited partnership. Like the S-Corporation, the LLC is appealing in that you have gained profits that place you in a high tax base and want to be able to cover the income with losses you usually anticipate in your first years in an enterprise. 20yrs ago, when I founded my first business company, my husband and I chose the S company. Both of us had salary income that put us in a high degree of taxes, and we realized that our new consultancy firm would incur substantial capital expenditures in the first few years. After all, we have to buy new devices, such as a fax machine, a laser printer, personal computers, and replaceable supplies. We were also conscious that building a list of customer would take a few years to get our profits out of business. The losses have been deducted from our total personal income, and taxes have been reduced considerably.

Why do you bother with an LLC if you can get this benefit from an S-corporation? The LLC has many advantages over the S company:

1. First of all, LLC has no restrictions on who may be a member of the LLC by the S-corporation. Only persons, properties, certain trusts, and other S-corporations may belong to an S-corporation. Either US citizens or residents must be individuals (shareholders). The LLC is not, however, subject to these restrictions. It is thus an ideal entity, which you can combine with other entities in your organization. For example, a company or other legal entity may be an LLC member.

2. The LLC has much greater flexibility than the S-Corporation in the assignment of rights, revenues, and properties. In other words, each share of the stock has the same rights as any other share. The S-Corporation has only one class of stock. The distribution of income and properties is thus highly rigid. If Parties A and B are equal shareholders of a company and plan to divide their income of $10,000, then A and B shall obtain $5,000 each. This could not possibly be fair if one partner was far more involved and generated much more benefit than the other. The LLC provides A with $8,000 if its business operation produces 80% of its earnings, leaving B the remaining 20%, or $2,000. This can be particularly interesting in a relationship in which the amount of money and ongoing business operations that the partners contribute to the enterprise are substantially different.

3. The LLC does not experience the same corporate formalities as the S or C Company is required. While the LLC also needs to maintain adequate LLC records and bookkeeping, the LLC does not need supervision by an executive board and minutes of daily board meetings.

4. In general, the liquidation of an LLC is not a taxable case, unlike the S-corporation. As the personal and financial circumstances change over time, you may decide that it is no longer in your interest to maintain a company for your business. Once your company starts to make a regular profit after the reasonably high costs of the first or two years, you might determine that a C-corporation with a tax rate of a maximum of 25 percent will help you more (unless it is a personal service corporation). The liquidation would be a taxable occurrence if you act as an S Company and liquidate it by selling the liquidated assets to the

shareholder(s) at fair market value. This is not applicable to the LLC. This is among the factors that makes the LLC particularly attractive.

5. The principle of the charge order makes the LLC particularly successful for security of properties. This makes it an especially desirable property holding firm. The company should not be used to own real estate, so the court may grant shares in the company in the judgment if the corporation is issued. Management over the business means control over the property and you are effectively losing control over the property.

In comparison, a charge order, which is used by Limited Liability Corporations, only requires the plaintiff to collect income dividends from the benefit of the party or parties against whom the case was brought. The order does not grant voting rights or management authority. Thus, current administrators or representatives might actually vote not to allocate money, thus leaving the plaintiff without recourse; however, even though the funds were not allocated, the plaintiff would continue to pay income taxes. This gives the complainant a good opportunity to seek a settlement.

The LLC is obviously a strong tool to shield your properties from financial depredation. If you use it for the real estate holdings, you can make full use of this security by keeping each property in a separate LLC. Thus, if one LLC is targeted by financial predators, only one property is impacted by the operations.

Restricted Liability Corporation Drawbacks

Of course, the LLC has some drawbacks – otherwise many other appealing ways to structure the company wouldn't remain. Why couldn't the LLC be your best option?

1. Increased taxes in high taxation brackets for LLC members. Once the LLC has made a profit, the revenue flows to the individual members who are taxed directly on that revenue, unless they are completely excluded from the LLC. Members who are heavily taxed would also pay higher taxes than if they were using a C company subject to lower marginal tax rates. Proper preparation of expenditure disbursements and other business aspects could address that disadvantage.

2. In some states, there's higher initial filing fees for LLCs. Some countries can, in their early years, place heavier tax obligations on LLCs. Our country of California allows the LLC in its first year to make a minimum of $800 in tax, while businesses are exempt in their first year — whether they have any revenue or not! It can still be worth starting an LLC: if you have high start-up expenses, the higher filing fees will prevail over the thousands of dollars tax savings.

3. Unlike businesses, LLCs do not have continuity of existence and are usually limited to a certain period of time (say, 50 years) depending on the state. If a member of the LLC dies, the other members may vote to continue their business. LLC interests may be donated to other family members, and the LLC may as a member have a trust or family limited partnership, thereby ensuring successful property planning.

4. The LLC is an untested entity. There is the broad variety of corporate case law, but LLCs. We should also expect improvements in the laws regulating LLCs to become clearer to lawmakers about the ramifications of this new agency.

CHAPTER FIVE
Flexibility and Default Rules

A limited liability company which incorporates traditional corporate and partnership arrangements, is a highly versatile type of business arrangement. By establishing an LLC, you create a legal entity that provides its owners with limited liability. Sometimes they are mistakenly referred to as a limited liability partnership rather than a limited liability company. It is a truly hybrid business entity that can contain corporate elements and/or qualities, partnerships, and even sole ownership, depending on the number of owners involved. An LLC, while it is a company, is, in reality, a form of unincorporated company and not a company. The primary advantage of an LLC sharing with a company is the limited liability insurance provided by both. The key feature of an LLC sharing in a relationship is its passing income tax. However, it is much more versatile than an organization and is very good for individual owners.

You should recognize that either company or organization with limited liability does not always shield owners from liability. The legal system in the United States does allow a court system to pierce an LLC's corporate veil if any form of fraud or mistake occurs or if the owner uses the business as an 'alter ego.'

Rules of Flexibility and Default

All the LLC legal statutes contain a sentence similar to "except where otherwise provided for in the operating agreement," which gives the members of an LLC the flexibility to determine how their LLC is governed. Certain laws include default governance guidelines for an LLC, which apply unless an operating arrangement is reached.

Income Taxation

LLCs are regarded as a transitional agency by default for the purposes of the Internal Revenue Service and Federal Income Taxes. If there is only one owner, or shareholder the limited liability corporation is automatically considered a "non-owned entity" for the purposes of taxation, and the owner shall be required to declare the revenue of the LLC in its personal tax return under Schedule C. If the LLC has multiple members, it shall be regarded as corporeality and shall file IRS 1065. Partners earn K-1 so that they can register on their tax return for their share of losses or revenues.

LLCs can also choose to be taxed as an organization by simply submitting IRS form 8832. They will either be classified as a standard C company, or they may opt to be classified as an S-company. If regarded as a C-Corporation, before any dividends or distributions are paid to the members, the income of the company is taxable, and afterward, the taxation of the dividends or distributions shall be taxed as income to the members. Some experts recommended the LLC as an S-Corp as the best possible framework for small companies, as the LLC's versatility and simplicity are combined with S-Corp's self-employment income tax saving.

Advantages

Here are the characteristics that are most commonly seen as the benefits of a limited liability company:

- Check the tax box. LLCs can be taxed as a sole proprietor, company, S-Corporation, or C-Corporation, which offers a lot of versatility.
- Restricted liability. Limited liability. The owners of the LLC who are recognized as members are normally shielded from any or all liability in connection with the LLC's activities and debts, depending on state legislation in which the LLC was created.

- Administrative paperwork and record keeping in comparison with a company are greatly simplified.
- Tax passage is compulsory unless the LLC wishes to be taxed as a C-corporation.
- Profits would be charged on the individual member's level rather than on the LLC by actually using the IRS's default tax classification.
- LLCs are commonly regarded in most countries to be a fully different agency from the owners of the LLCs.

- LLC's may typically be formed with only one person involved.
- The LLC may grant its membership interests, and it may then distribute the economic advantages of these interests, thereby having the economic benefit of sharing the company's profit and losses, as in a partnership, without necessarily transferring the title to the interest.
- Even if the LLC has embraced a corporate tax structure, LLC's revenue typically remains in the hands of its members;
- Members may usually create their own governance and security protections for members by implementing an operating agreement.

Disadvantages

Here are the features of a limited liability partnership which are commonly known as disadvantages:

- Most countries have no constitutional requirement for an LLC to have an operating agreement, but you could be in trouble if you are a multi-member LLC member unless you have an operating agreement because most countries do not dictate the governance of and security of members of LLC just as they would do for a regular company.
- It is not that easy for a member to sell its interest in a limited liability company even if the LLC is held by more than one member, as the LLC cannot issue or sell stock certificates.
- Certain investors would make investments in companies more secure because of the prospect of an eventual IPO. This can make raising financial resources more challenging.
- Franchise taxes on LLCs are imposed in many countries. This tax is simply a levy that LLC pays for limited liability to the state. This tax may be based on wages, earnings, number of owners, volume, or a combination of capital employed in the state.
- LLCs in the District of Columbia are regarded as taxable entities that exclude the advantages of pass-through taxation.

- Renovation or annual payments in certain countries can be higher than companies.
- The creditors are known to compel LLC members to sign and guarantee LLC's personal debts, clearly making the debt liable to their owners.

Variations
- The LLC series is a rare and unique type of LLC. It enables a single LLC to divide its assets into different sequences.
- A LLC Specialist, also known as a PLLC, PLLC, or PL, is an LLC form specially created for the purposes of delivering a professional service. This typically includes occupations in which the state requires a license, for example, a doctor, chiropractor, lawyer, accountant, architect, or engineer, for delivering those same services. Some countries do not allow an LLC to engage in a licensed professional practice.

Series LLC - Where Angels Fear to Tread

There's a lot of speculation about LLC episodes. More and more people are asking if they are an intelligent idea. The short response is that you are not, you were not checked, and you have minimal applications if you have any.

First of all, a certain history. For several different applications, LLCs alone is an excellent framework. For example, they function as well as a means of keeping high-dollar assets such as real estate. It is necessary to hold titles to that property in an entity, whether you own a commercial or rental property. If the organization (most possibly an LLC) is properly run and managed, it will protect you from any personal obligations.

Many people have numerous investment assets. By putting them in one or more LLCs, they want to secure their savings and themselves. The job is then a scenario; all investments are placed under another LLC. This is not a common response for people who have many savings, but it is focused on sound logic. Consider LLCs as giant boxes. As many investment products as you like can be added, but if anything happens in the event, they are all in danger. Any money you put in that LLC will be in danger if a lawsuit occurs.

The way to differentiate your assets is you should preferably use a separate LLC for each. If you can't, be sure to analyze your equity, along with your liability potential, in each investment. Then group them accordingly in LLCs. For instance, it is not a good idea to include in the same LLC a single-family beach rental in Maui as a duplex on the wrong side of the city. You might have thousands of dollars of equity in the house of Maui, which is jeopardized by the same LLC as the rough-edged duplex. Keep them apart. Keep them apart. However, if you own three single-family homes in Idaho, and each one has equity of about twenty thousand dollars, it may be a reasonable risk to put them together. But the tactic of segregation can be costly.

If you have ten properties, it might seem overwhelming and expensive to use ten separate LLCs. The LLC series seems to be a solution as laws in some countries allow you to establish separate series within a single LLC, which only impose debts and liabilities against that series. These laws permit LLCs to create separate interests, members, and managers and to provide them with separate responsibilities, powers, and rights. This includes the rights to gains and losses on such property and commitments. Each series within the LLC acts as a separate state agency in states with this form of enabling legislation. That is why many people are drawn to series LLCs — technically, they have the potential to defend property from debt accrued in or against each other in various series without paying government fees for multiple entities. Thus, an LLC containing two properties can choose to position each in a separate sequence so that one's liabilities cannot cause problems in the other's assets. (Remember that two separate LLCs can have the same effect.) Many people choose LLCs because they seem cheaper to set up at first glance. This assumption, however, is incorrect. In fact, the setting up of an LLC series is more complicated and costly than the simple one. In California, you might find an LLC series appealing because each company is paid an annual fee of $800 by the Franchise Tax Board. Many people assume that setting up a single LLC series means in California paying only one bill. However, it is the position of the Franchise Tax Board that each series has its own LLC for payment purposes, which ensures that you will be paying the same, whether you have set up assets in series or in your own separate LLCs.

The key issue with the LLC series is that many states (including California) do not have series legislation and can choose to disregard the legislation of the state in which the series was created. That's because when you do business in your state, you are subject to their rules. The California Franchise Tax Board's example of attitude is applicable to fees, but obligation protection is also an issue. Because the LLC series is so new, the courts have never tested them, even in states that allow them. This means that no assurance can be provided that limited liability rights will be applied to every sequence before all state laws apply. It is difficult to see if a court can grant this kind of defense within an agency, and only time can tell if the courts would. But would you like this kind of confusion when you try to secure your assets?

Again, one should be worried about how the states that have no laws authorizing them would handle LLCs in sequence. When you create an LLC series in Nevada, then register it as a foreign company in the state of Massachusetts, each LLC series has a separate part of its property. If a case is brought against one of them, you can't be sure that the Massachusetts Court will stick to the LLC's series framework and extend Nevada's law to the Massachusetts property and activities. If so, the claimant can only collect for the property in that order. If not, the applicant can also collect properties in other series. States are supposed to give full a faith and credit to other states' laws, but the response is unclear. Exceptions do happen. It is also important to remember that the American Bar Association reviewed and refused to approve the sequence of LLCs. You can rest assured that this development will be noted in future court cases.

As the laws concerning the development of LLCs in each country are different, it could take a long time before enough of the jurisprudence is accumulated to give us some comfort in using them. If you want to ensure that your assets have decent, strong security, it is much better not to provide reliable protection to corporate structures. Avoid series LLCs as a means of defense before the case law has been established and instead depend on known tested entities like individual LLCs.

The Wrong Business Structure Can Destroy Your Financial Future

You have a lot of responsibility when running a company and offering a product or service as a sole proprietorship. The second worst form of asset security after a general partnership is a sole proprietorship. A general partnership as a corporate structure is not good since all eight doctors are responsible for the wrongdoings of one of their partners in a combined medical practice.

The situation isn't any better in one-stop shop, since you might lose your company as well as your home, vehicles and everything else if you are sued and eventually judged for damages against you. Businessmen are using a C company or a S corporation for asset security, as the judgment owner might be able to get your business but cannot get your personal assets when prosecuted in the same case (in view of a judgment).

The main distinction between a C Corp and an S Corp is that the tax effects of the corporation pass on your personal tax return in an S Corp. If you start up business or run a small business, it rarely works because lenders won't lend you cash into a C Corp or S Corp without you directly guaranteeing your bill.

Therefore, asset security is not automatic in a C Corp or S Corp. The veil of the business (so to speak) is far more than it protects. It is preferred a limited liability company (LLC), which is not an LLC, but has other members, and you manage the LLC as its owner.

Under this arrangement you are far more liable than a C Corp or S Corp because it might not be automatic to pay a judgment against you. You can increase your security of assets when creating your LLC with accompanying training articles if you insert a judgment creditor's clause in your articles. In several countries, you will obtain more security from properties.

When searching for the last time, about half of the countries permit a judgment creditor clause and half (California being one).

The implementation of a judgment creditor clause does not impact your case or your judgment. What a judgment creditor clause does is ask if the LLC created in this way can pay the judgment promptly. If the manager of the LLC paying the judgment will, in the clear discretion of the manager, paralyze or kill the LLC in its activities, then the judgment shall not be paid until the LLC disbands and the judgment shall at that point pay the residual properties.

Why? Since the other LLC members with equity interest who had nothing to do with being a proceedings party against one LLC member will be affected and their rights must be safeguarded by payment of the judgment. You may want to know that the Internal Revenue Service (IRS) does not accept LLC as a business structure in itself, but only as a company.

Therefore, when creating an LLC (single-person company) as a single-person company, you will file a tax form different to that when setting up an LLC with members, you would submit a Form 1065. You would not have the same security when creating a solo LLC as if creating an LLC with members.

When asking an attorney about the best way to protect assets and he or she says that I buy an insurance policy, can't easily run in the opposite direction. Their response is their interpretation of the subject.

I considered the vast majority of lawyers to be very useless, as their knowledge of asset security issues is at best marginal. It's my impression that many lawyers are either so busy making their second million or just trying to survive in practice that they don't have time or interest to keep up with their career.

Professionals in this role are consumed by the need to pay their bills or develop ample wealth to retire early. If you want to have fun, open the yellow pages on your local phone book and the listing where the lawyers pay to be placed in a certain category (such as corporate law and divorce actions)

I did this in a region of over 500 000 people and there was not even an asset security group, much less a single list. Asset defense is not a commonly practiced field of law, much less known by many lawyers

Two of my customers each set up their own LLC with a 95 percent share and another with a 5 percent stake. Both were the 5 percent equity interest of each other because they were neither married, nor had a significant other, nor children.

Real Estate Tax Strategies and Forming an LLC

The first step in making any investment in real estate is to start a company. There are different types of business entities: Limited Liability Company (LLC), sole proprietorship, Limited Liability Partnership (LLP), Series LLC (only in certain states), S-Corp, LLLP, C-Corp. Series LLC can be set up in the following states: Delaware, Oklahoma, Iowa, Utah, Tennessee, Wisconsin.

They all have their benefits and drawbacks. Limited Liability Company is the only real tax corporation flow and is the most advantageous one for holding immovable property. The Limited Liability Corporation helps you to pay pre-tax business expenses. It is really important to remember that your taxes have been deducted when you get paid and collect your paycheck, and all your expenses, whether related to a property or company, are deducted on an AFTER TAX basis. If you have an LLC, you take all company spending, subtract it and pay income tax on what is left. LLC needs no records of meetings and minutes. Documentation is restricted to the organization's papers listed by LLC members.

LLC is a pass and, if it is a single member, the corporation is found not to be taken into account by the IRS. A business is subject to double taxation if not only earnings are taxed, but even the payment is taxed in the form of dividends. The other advantage is flexibility with respect to the transition of LLC ownership. Ownership in LLC is guided by an internal document of the Operating Agreement. Everything that needs to be done is the operating agreement in order to change ownership, and no entries are needed other than changes with the IRS for a given tax ID number. LLC is the only organization not restricted to defeat! It also has fewer filings than an S-Corp and is very easy to retain. If you have several properties, have them in LLC and have one LLC that will own all the other LLCs. Your primary holding LLC is a single member of LLC for the other holdings for tax purposes, and you will have to file only one tax return. In addition to the tax advantages, LLC also offers a simple degree of asset protection. If the corporation owns the properties, they are separate from the personal assets and cannot be harmed in case of a lawsuit. Please note that LLC is an asset defense BASIC level, and if the opponent has a good lawyer, there are several ways to make your personal assets a part of legal action. It is called the corporate veil piercing. For instance, you must have a separate LLC bank account. If your LLC owns your house, then all house relates to income and expenditures from the bank account in question. If not, the status of the LLC will be excluded, and the personal assets will be included in the lawsuit. Your LLC must be in good faith with the state, and your organization article must be properly notified. The object of the company must be explicitly defined without exclusions, and, where necessary, you must request amendments. If you purchase real estate, you have to tell you to purchase, keep, sell or rent land; if you buy property, you have to tell that you buy for profit, etc. In certain countries, LLCs need to be released, which can be very costly; in other nations, including Maryland, you need to pay an annual fee of $300 a year. You must review your claims and rules and stay with the state at all times.

Main Residence. If you have the LLC, you might need an office, and it could be in your own personal home conveniently enough. You can subtract rental payments for your office space in your personal residence, according to IRS Code 288G.

Depreciation. It is the most advantageous real estate deduction! Although the property is worthwhile, you will depreciate the property for the lifespan of the house, which is 27.5 years, and you are deducted from the profits. However, only the house can be depreciated; the property cannot be depreciated. For example, if you buy a house of 100,000, the building's value will only be $80,000, and the land's value $20,000. You should then only recognize depreciation costs against the value of the house.

Depreciation accelerated. You may have heard from your accountant that accelerated depreciation for real estate is not approved, but there is a way to make changes deducted in previous years. For example, over 15 years of land improvements such as curbs, sidewalks, and landscaping have been decreased; personal property has been depreciated by five years. Objects considered as personal property under IRS 1.48-1(c) shall have one of the following characteristics;
1. Accessory
2. Function
3. Movability.

Basically, all the accessories, features, or movables are real estate. When you do rehabilitation and can install mobile walls, the costs of upgrades can be deducted for five years. You would have to take 5-6 times less deduction for progress in the next five years if they are not mobile. Let it all work, be an accessory, or let it mobile! A company developer designed his office building with lightweight mobile walls and could subtract 80,000 dollars the same year.

Status of DEALER. It is necessary to avoid the "DEALER" status when flipping assets. In certain cases, it can be avoided by flipping assets by various companies, in certain cases, through a couple of transactions, but simply stating your INVESTMENT INTENT is the simplest 'investor-friendly' way. If you state that your investment intent is buying, holding, leasing, or renting assets without being required to sell under such circumstances such as working capital, you can get away from not being involved.

Red Flags IRS. Also, you shouldn't do those activities that raise red flags to the IRS because you may be audited. Next, don't declare too much loss of rental income; there are plenty of expenditures to reduce your earnings before tax. Second, don't make your asset security structure more difficult. For too many companies upside down or with headquarters in Las Vegas, NV, a tax-free state could be a red flag. Red flags are still raised for disclosing losses for more than two years. The common sense behind it: "Why are you still doing business because you make money?" Excessive contributions, high costs compared with high income can also lead to an audit.

Taxes on land. Investors of real estate are subject to a variety of taxes, including land taxes. The property's measured worth and market value still have a difference. In 2007 the value was generally lower and 99% higher than the market value of the property in 2010. Taxes are not necessarily reassessed according to the business cycle, and you have to challenge them. In the State of Maryland, personal property taxes can be disputed for the next year's hearing within 60 days of the date of settlement or file before year-end. Even though taxes constitute a deduction from profits, they are not tax credits, and the more benefit you can minimize. To challenge your tax bill successfully, you must demonstrate comparable and recent real estate sales prices in your town. You would also have to equate the recently sold property with the number of bedrooms, bathrooms, square feet, services, etc.

Taxes on capital gains. This form of tax is only levied when the property is sold. This tax refers to the disparity between the selling price and the sales price. Homeowners residing on the property for at least two years and the sum of benefits are excluded. There is a way to postpone taxes on capital gains by swapping 1031. Make sure you contact an escrow firm and do it in compliance with the IRS guidelines. In compliance with this IRS law, you can sell your house, locate another house, bid within 45 days, and agree on a new property within six months. According to the IRS tax laws, the property you buy must be a 'like' property that does not matter if it's bigger, as long as the property you just sold is an 'investment.' You can then purchase a single-family house and buy a flat as long as these were investment properties.

What is important to know before an LLC is set up?

Your corporation should be on behalf of your LLC. Many companies name LLC at the street address, like 17 Lexington Ave LLC. I prefer to name them by number and street name only without St.. Ave.. Ct.. etc For example 17 Lexington LLC. When you set up a number of LLCs, it becomes unclear which was St or Ave, and the right orthography of the LLC is completely important in everything you do.

CHECKING NAME AVAILABILITY. You need to consult with the Secretary of State until you select the name. In certain countries, you can do it online, and you can verify it there if you go to the Secretary of State. I like to go personally and file all papers, just so I can do it all right there and get all records in my hands on the same day. In MD, the expedited service costs extra, but it's worth paying because you need to get your bank account fixed immediately and everything else.

ORGANIZATIONAL POSTS. Organizational Posts include name, records, identifying LLC members and managers. At least in MD and NY, it does not have to be registered with the authority.

REGISTERED AGENT OR RESIDENT AGENT. An LLC is requested to work on behalf of the LLC by a resident agent. It can be a company or person residing in the state where LLC was formed. You may list your name and address, for instance, as a registered agent in New York, or employ a company to represent the LLC. If the LLC is established in a different state, a registered agent must be present in that state.

MISTAKES WHEN SETTING UP LLC:

1. *Start without a budget.* It is important to include a budget to set up an LLC, which requires filing fees, fees to hold an LLC (in the State of Maryland's assessment and tax department, $300 annual payment was necessary to keep LLC

in good standing), fees that the accountant would charge, additional taxes at year-end, some states require LLC to be released, and it may be extremely onerous (e.g., in New York and other countries).

2. *Do not want to verify the availability of the name.* It is important to verify the availability of LLC names before filing and paying the fee that could not be reimbursed! Not only would you probably have the same LLC name if you file paperwork where the title is transferred to the property, and that may become an issue.

3. *Always employ a prosecutor.* It is not accurate that only a lawyer can file and write paperwork. All should be entitled to apply for LLC, and legal fees are, in many cases, unnecessary.

4. *.Neglect other records.* Documents have to be reviewed to check they are appropriate and filed in each state, and it is YOUR duty to check even though you are hiring a specialist to do this for you.

5. *Contribute to several Capital-may not be a good idea.* Each state must contribute a minimum sum to the LLC. Only this amount or what you need to contribute is important because it is the distribution of the capital that is a taxable event to the IRS if you have to withdraw the funds.

6. *BUY-SELL DEAL SKIP.* An exit strategy is important, particularly if LLC is a partnership because you never know what will go wrong, and it is always easier to have everything published.

7. *GETTING TAX ID LATER* isn't a good idea since anything, including a bank account, should be obtained immediately. You can have a bank account without a tax ID, and without a separate bank account, IRS can ignore LLC as a company

8. *Only tax the ballpark.* Never guess what your revenue and expenditures are, and report them correctly. If your property has a separate LLC account, enter checks for all costs, including repairs, government charges, property taxes, administration fees and all other costs related to the property from the LLC account.

9. Using an LLC personal benefit account is completely unethical, and very expensive. Where LLC has not been used for the purposes of the operating contract alone and does not include similar expenditures, the status of the LLC may be disregarded, and you may be responsible for the lawyer's litigation.

CHAPTER SIX
Entity Formation Fundamentals

Among the most critical steps in any fiscal plan is to decide what company and investments should be created. Four main categories of companies exist for legal purposes: sole ownership, partnership, business, and limited company liability. The body you select should take both the tax consequences of the body and the legal aspects of the body into account.

-Sole Proprietorship-

Let's explore each entity's fiscal and legal aspects, starting with sole ownership. A single corporation isn't even an agency. It's what happens if you don't have an agency and no partners. The simplest type of business is sole ownership. You actually record your income in your personal income tax return in Schedule C. No balance sheet and only a small income statement must be held. Sounds amazing, right? This is one of the worst business forms from a tax as well as a legal point of view.

From a tax standpoint, you will not only pay payroll taxes on all your payroll at your highest marginal rate, but will also pay 100% self-employment taxes. And you will be audited by the IRS at least 4 times more than any other corporate structure. If you have no loss in your sector, you'll pay the highest tax rate in a single corporation.

If it's not bad enough, the legal side of a single owner is worse. You are not only responsible for all your acts but also personally responsible for all your employees' acts. Don't take our word for it; ask your lawyer. They will confirm that a single owner does NOT have wealth protection.

So when are you going to use a single property? ALMOST NEVER. The only time you want to use a sole proprietorship is for a side company, where you are the only owner, the only worker and there is very little to no taxable income. However, if you use a single property as a result of low taxable profits or even losses, consider using an LLC for legal purposes – it may also be a sole proprietorship for tax purposes. LLCs are further discussed below.

-Partnerships-

Two types of partnerships exist for tax purposes: general partnerships and limited partnerships. The simplest type of partnership is general partnerships. Two or more individuals share both the management and financial duties of the partnership in a general partnership. Only general partners share management and financial roles in a limited partnership. Passive investors are the limited partners.

For tax purposes, the partnership revenue and deductions are reported in Form 1065, which is a separate tax return only for partnerships. Each partner receives a K-1 form which shows their share of each revenue or loss item. Revenue or loss from your K-1 is recorded in your return on personal income tax. The partnership usually does not pay income tax. Partnership dividends are not usually taxed to the spouses.

General partners are usually responsible for all relationship debts. This means you will lose more than the amount you spent. When the partnership is litigated, the general partners are usually "at the hook" for decisions greater than the partnership it will pay. Restricted partners are usually only responsible for the amount of their actual investment.

General partners must pay social security taxes on their share of the partnership's ordinary income. Restricted partners usually have no social security tax on their share of the partnership's profits.

-Corporations-

There are two types of corporations for tax purposes: S corporations and C corporations. S companies like partnerships are taxed a lot. The income is indicated on a separate tax return, 1120S, and the shareholders receive a K-1 showing their share of each income or loss item. Revenue or loss from your K-1 is recorded in your return on personal income tax. The S business usually does not pay income tax. S corporate dividends are usually not charged by the shareholder. Moreover, social security taxes are not usually applied.

C businesses are different. C companies have their own collection of tax rules, tax rates and pay their own taxes. They report their revenue on a 1120 form and pay tax directly to the IRS. C company owners are subject to tax only on dividends from the company. These distributions are known as dividends, often taxed at lower rates than other wages.

Corporate shareholders are not usually responsible for the company's debts unless they have pledged the debt directly. This means that shareholders will typically only lose the amount they invested in the company

—Limited Liability Companies-

For tax purposes, corporations with limited liability may be taxed as any tax agency that the owners wish. The IRS permits a limited liability corporation to determine how to tax it. There are some basic rules surrounding the taxation of LLCs.

LLC's, with only one owner, are typically taxed as single ownerships. The IRS considers this a "disregarded entity." The LLC is also ignored for tax purposes. The owner of the LLC can, however, choose to bill the LLC as a C company or an S company (subject to the S corporation ownership rules).

Multi-member LLCs are typically taxed as partnerships of two or more owners. Depending on the obligations of the individual members (owners), these can be paid either as a general partnership or as a limited partnership. However, the LLC owners can choose to have the LLC taxed as a C company or as an S company (subject to S company property rules). The taxation of distributions from LLC depends entirely on how members want to tax the LLC, that is as a partnership, an S corporation or a C corporation, and obey the distribution rules of the tax body.

Like a business, LLC owners are usually not responsible for the company's debts unless they guarantee the debt in their own right. This means that LLC members will usually only lose the amount that they have invested in the company.

Financial Privacy Using Legal Entities

A Separate Legal Person

Legal entities are outstanding legal entities by their design, broad recognition under the law, and tax treatment to protect your privacy and preserve ownership of property in a way that offers a lower profile and helps improve the protection of personal and financial privacy.

In my first book on privacy, we discussed the increasing danger of identity theft and the dreadful trend towards fraud and robbery in America, and we discussed several preventive strategies. A few years later, my second book on privacy looked at the problem of using legal entities as tactical means to keep land ownership to divert your attention from personal interests, reduce the risk of losses due to personal liability and help to manage and strengthen your personal financial privacy. I would like to choose three particular legal entities for their privacy concerns in this article:

- Corporations
- Limited Liability Companies
- Triple LPs

They all share the fact that they are legal entities recognized by the States which use statutory protection. Each is treated as a separate legal individual from its owners. Apart from its owners, each one can have a separate identity and tax life. Each was recognized not only by statutory law but also by tax law and under review by the Court.

Although each corporation, the limited liability company, and the limited liability partnership have been examined separately in terms of their business usage and their asset security utilities, each one of them shall only be examined in terms of privacy.

Using a Low-Profile Corporation

Corporations were with us for a long time. They come from the English common law tradition and are commonly used in the USA. A business is defined as an artificial legal entity that is treated as a separate legal entity. Similar to a normal individual, the organization can have land, enter into contracts, recruit and fire workers, open and retain bank accounts, and use courts to obtain redress and defend itself.

One benefit is that the owners of a company (which is known as shareholders) usually have no personal responsibility for their liabilities and debts (except that the IRS may charge shareholders the unpaid taxes of a company). Any lucrative business starts life as a so-called "C" business and is taxed separately from its shareholders. Some of them are eventually taxed under subchapter 'S' of the Internal Revenue Code and then taxed as tax entities, i.e., their benefit is taxed federally and registered on the owners' personal income tax returns. For several years in the late 20th century, 'S' was the knee-jerk method taken by several consultants.

From a privacy point of view, a private business (one that has not become 'public') may be used to establish a lower profile. If the company, for example, does not have a personal name attached (i.e. 'The John Alfred Jones Corporation') and uses a trading name (i.e. 'Green River Lending, Inc.), your personal identity does not draw attention to your personal identity and sensibilities to the company.

Without your specific identity and financial status, the company could have bank accounts, cars, investment accounts, trademarks, copyright, patents, and other properties under its name.

LLCs and Financial Privacy

By its lawful nature, an LLC is an ownership arrangement that allows its owner (called 'Members') to benefit by minimizing their personal liability risk and, at the same time, provides them with tax benefits more similar to that of a partnership in which the company's profit is passed to the owner and taxed on income tax returns.

An LLC is a different artificial legal 'individual.' As a company, the company will own bank accounts, investment securities, land, office buildings, residential property, mutual funds, stock trading accounts, option accounts, commodity trading accounts, and intellectual properties as well.

The assets kept on behalf of the LLC are more private. It is less likely to have access to properties or accounts on behalf of the LLC than an identity thief. This helps you to have a lower profile and increases your personal financial protection since property ownership of the company does not actually disclose your personal identity itself.

Private Triple LPs

All 50 countries now have limited partnerships under their laws. A limited partnership is an arrangement that allows its members to benefit from a limited personal responsibility for the partnership's debts and liabilities. The general partners have unlimited criminal responsibility in the majority of countries. In an increasing minority of countries, however, the trend is for general partners to also benefit from a more advanced form of liability security called the limited liability limited partnership.

The main difference between the general partner and the position of the limited partner is that of day-to-day management and decision-making. The partnership is run by the general partners and take regular operating and investment decisions. On the other hand, the limited partners are passive investors who cannot make business decisions.

The more sophisticated variant - the Limited Liability Limited Partnership (also known as 'LLLP' or the 'Triple LP') - entitles the general partner to limited liability and may own land in the same private manner as companies and LLCs. Your personal name is not with the name of the partnership on properties. With this relationship being the owner of investment accounts, including, for example, an inventory or options trading account, it is much less likely that an identity thief will even have far less access to the account.

The argument, of course, is that not understanding the nature of the account – kept under a name other than yours – is much less practical and prevents you far more than you might otherwise be if you were illegal to have access to it.

Common Business Structures

A Single Property is a one-person business. There is no paperwork to complete. The benefit or loss from the company is passed to the Sole Proprietor's personal tax return. The sole owner is responsible for all the company's debts and other liabilities.

In most countries, fictitious name registration (DBA) is required. You must register your fictitious name before beginning your business activity. In certain cases, the transaction must be done within 30-40 days of the first transaction. Moreover, some states require you to publish in a local newspaper your DBA declaration and to file evidence with the appropriate government bureau. The aim of the publication requirement is to ensure that new firms, their legal name, and ownership are informed to the public.

A relationship requires two or more individuals. The benefit or loss is split among the partners and is recorded in their personal tax returns. Each partner shall be directly responsible for the company's debts or other liabilities.

A corporation is a distinct and separate legal body. This means that a corporation can open a bank account, own property, and conduct business under its own name. Corporations are regulated by a Board of Directors that makes significant business decisions and manages the corporation's general businesses.

The directors are chosen by the company's shareholders. Directors are named by officers who perform the day-to-day activities of the company.

The corporation's principal benefit is that its members, known as shareholders are not directly responsible for any of the corporation's debts or obligations. In the majority of cases, for example, if a company is sued or forced into bankruptcy, the creditors would not be expected to settle the debt with their own money if the company's assets are not enough to cover the liabilities. In most cases, the creditor cannot reclaim any loss after the owners, administrators, or officers of the company.

Company owners also lost everything they had if the new business went poorly. The investors had to make a difference with their own money because the company was out of money, and they did not have the money to pay creditors. By establishing a corporation, investors could escape this type of liability, and more people are more prepared to invest their money in business projects. The incorporation of a Company as a corporate organization will help you minimize taxes, but above all, you will protect your personal assets by maintaining peace of mind.

There are two corporate forms. The IRS permits a corporation to be taxed as a C corporation or an S company.

Profits of a C business are taxed on two occasions, generally known as double taxation. A C corporation pays the corporate income tax and then distributes earnings as a dividend to shareholders paying income tax on those dividends.

The avoidance of double taxation by a C company is by making a special option with the IRS to be levied as an S corporation. This means that the income is taxed as a partnership or as a single owner. There is only one degree of taxation in this manner. Corporate gains and losses are transferred to owners who instead pay the benefit taxes at individual personal tax rates. You may use income changes to benefit from lower taxes.

Let's see an example:

For this example, we assume that ABC Company is a single ownership and has $100,000 in revenue. As a single owner, the tax rate is 25%. If it were instead ABC Company, presume business owner earns $50,000 in pay and leaves $50,000 in benefit. The federal income tax rate is (15% of $50,000) and the personal tax rate (15% of $50,000). This is a strong benefit of establishing a corporation.

Other Benefits:

Corporations should provide workers with compensation packages. You can rent your company properties. The corporation pays a rental fee and can claim rental income and expenses, including interest, depreciation, repairs, maintenance, insurance, and expenses.

In a corporation, the amount of capital or operating losses that a corporation is permitted to carry back or forward to subsequent fiscal years are not limited. Unless a single owner compensates for capital losses, the owner cannot report a capital loss of $3,000.

The money gained by the single owner is taxed on self-employment. The taxes actually amount to 13.3 percent on the first income of $106,800. In a corporation, only wages are subject to such taxes and not income. You will save thousands of dollars annually.

Let's look at a different example:

When a single owner gains $80,000, the entire $80,000 will have to pay a tax of 13.3%. Let us suppose that the organization already receives $80,000, but that $35,000 is paid as a wage. In this scenario, $45,000 is called its benefit; its tax on self-employment will not be charged on a benefit of $45,000. This saves you more than $5,000 annually. It is very important to remember that you can pay a fair wage and benefit from all tax benefits provided by a company. But don't forget that there are corporate ownership obligations, and the Corporate Book is perhaps the most important. We're going to talk about it later.

Each business structure has differences, and the one that best suits your business's needs should be selected. Taxation is the main difference between

Single Ownership, Partnership, or DBA and the company. Before deciding which business framework to use, you want to determine both the strengths and weaknesses. Note that a single owner or investor in a corporation is responsible for all the business costs. This ensures that all company debts are still responsible.

An S Company helps to prevent duplication of taxes. This happens where the benefit of the corporation is taxed, and the dividends are sent to the shareholders and taxed to the personal tax return of the shareholder. The most important thing to note is that a C company and an S company will protect you from corporate liabilities. A single owner or partnership partner is directly liable for company debts. In an organization, shareholders are not responsible for the bulk of corporate debts or liabilities if the company fails.

The Corporate Book is an important subject to explore. It is a three-ring binder that records all of the company's transactions or meetings. This means from opening a bank account to selling real estate. The Corporate Book is the key responsibility of the organization. The corporate book is generally managed by the secretary or treasurer of the company. You might potentially lose your status as a company without recording a corporate book and be subject to the required tax. This is called the corporate veil piercing.

Individual shareholders can, in certain conditions, be liable for corporate debts; for example, in situations where the shareholder guarantees a corporate debt, they or he will be responsible for that debt if the company fails. If corporate funds are mixed with personal capital, this enables you to pierce the corporate veil. The Corporate Book cannot even be documented to allow the veil to pierce. This means that shareholders would be personally responsible for all of the corporation's debts and other liabilities. There are strict corporate rules and regulations, and the important thing is to keep the Corporate Book.

The limited liability company has been created by corporations who wish to bypass the rules of a corporation. The LLC was formed to shield the owners of the company from personal liability if the company failed. It's a form of business organization that combines the security of a corporation's personal responsibility with fiscal benefits and relationship simplicity.

The LLC has the same tax advantages as the S Company with limited responsibility on corporate debts. The owners are named Members. The number of members permitted is not limited. LLC operates in a similar way to associations with flexibility and tax contributions on income to Members' personal tax returns.

An LIC is a form of corporate ownership that incorporates many characteristics of corporate and corporate structures. It's not a business. Owners are not appointed associates or shareholders. The number of members is unlimited and can include individuals, businesses, or other LLCs.

Members of an LLC are covered by a corporation's liability. Members shall not be held directly responsible for debts until a personal pledge is signed. An LLC exists like an organization as a separate entity.

Limited liability corporations can choose different types of benefit sharing. In comparison to a joint relationship with x / x split, the LLC is even more flexible. The framework of LLC does not need Minutes or Resolutions Corporate Book and is simpler to run than a corporation.

All the business losses, profits, and costs go to individual members through the organization. Double taxation of corporate and personal taxes is avoided. Companies will survive indefinitely, whereas the LLC is dissolved when a member dies or fails. Members who want to buy their public company or issue their employee shares in the future could be better served by selecting a corporate structure.

Single ownership or alliances can be less burdensome and less complicated. An LLC can, for tax purposes, be federally listed as a sole proprietor, partnership, or company. Classification may be chosen, or a default may be requested.

The formation of an LLC may not be as easy as a single entity, but the process is far smaller than a corporation. Two steps are taken to become an LLC;

1. Articles of Organization: You will be required to file the Articles of Organization with the Secretary of State if you intend to form a limited liability corporation and pay the required fees.

2. Operating Agreement: The operating agreement specifies the corporate agreements such as benefit-sharing, ownership, obligations, and alteration of

ownership. Each State has different rules for the establishment of a limited liability company. Some states want to tell the local newspaper about the establishment of a corporation.

The individual State Law establishes an LLC. The IRS uses the definition of a tax body, which enables the LLC to be regarded as a corporation, business, sole owner depending on the LLC election and the number of members.

Multi-member LLCs may be a partnership or a corporation, including S. A LLC must file Form 8832 Election for Entity Registration and elect to be taxed as a corporation. A multi-member LLC that does not want to do so will be listed as a partnership and taxed in compliance with federal legislation.

Choosing a Business Entity

Perhaps you have just chosen to start a new company from scratch, or perhaps a hobby of yours has matured over the years to make money. For your experience, service, or handicraft, people come to you and pay you for it. Cash is easy to manage, but then you have begun to accept checks made on your own behalf and transfers from PayPal connected to your personal bank account. Now it has gone beyond how casually you can account for your profits, so you intend to formalize your business. Do you have a single owner, a partnership, a limited liability corporation, or an S or C corporation? In this chapter, we will address some of the benefits and drawbacks of the different options of companies to help you decide what is right for you. It can always be modified later, but it takes time, effort, and resources, so it is best to prepare ahead on a long-term basis.

The simplest type of business is you, under your own name, do the work; it's called sole ownership. You should be responsible for your company's sales and expenditures; however, you can get your own funds. Save your expenses receipts and keep a record of your taxes. If your company is tiny, it's probably the best option because you have no additional red tape or bureaucracy – you don't have to register your corporation, you probably don't need a lawyer or an accountant, and you can still use the business costs as a tax deduction in your IRS Schedule C for more years as long as you make more profit than you can.

If in the municipalities where you sell your goods or service is taxable, you may have to register with the state or local tax office to collect and send sales and use tax on the products and services you sell. You retain a small amount of the sales tax you collect here in New York to make up for the paperwork and recordkeeping that has been completed. If you conduct value-added services on taxable products of another, such as the completion or reselling of unfinished birdhouses, you can receive a 'resale' permit to supply your suppliers so that the sales tax on the intermediary items that you buy for resale is not paid. If you buy a $10 unfinished birdhouse, you will not pay sales tax on it, but you will collect and pay sales tax on that price from the user if you resell it for $20. Remember that you are the customer of paintbrushes that you use to paint birdhouses; the income tax bill can be deducted from the benefit, but you still have to pay sales tax.

There are a few ways of creating a single company; as described, you can easily use your own social security number under your own name. If you prefer to name your business separately (called "doing business as" or "DBA"), please contact your county clerk for the process. To set up separate tax identifiers for your company (called 'taxpayer identification number,' 'employer identification number,' 'TIN,' or 'EIN'), contact the IRS or visit their form on their website. A DBA is usually charged, but a TIN or EIN is free. After you have obtained DBA documents, bring a copy to your bank to open an account on behalf of your company. The sole proprietorship provides many benefits, including business expense deductions, and allows you to create a separate company to perform business activities while minimizing your paperwork and your legal & accounting costs. The downside is that you are the corporation – there is no legal or financial difference between the duties of the company and your own. You are legally liable when your product injures someone or damages property during service performance. If the corporation undertakes contractual commitments it cannot recover, the creditors will persecute you personally.

The next party to be considered is collaboration. In some ways, this is better than ownership alone, but in some ways, it is worse. Collaboration is essentially a joint undertaking between you and one or more others. All will spend as much as agreed, work as much as possible and benefit as agreed. It is certainly the safest thing to create a separate tax ID and a "doing business" for this form of agreement (rather than using any partner's own name). If you carry your DBA paperwork into the bank to open accounts, you decide who has the right to sign checks and how many signatures are required for each check. The great benefit of collaboration is that together you can do more; you share management obligations and have a broader capital pool than everyone has individually. The downside is that every partner has complete authority to engage the company in responsibilities for which each partner is jointly and severally responsible. This means that your husband can sign up for magazines, sign up for the mobile plan, or take up a loan, and the creditors can come after you for the money if he stops paying. When your partner disappears, it is much easier for them to make a decision on levying investments, receiving your income, or linking to your property than on their absent partner. On the other hand, it is always difficult to find good assistance, so if you and two friends wish to open an appointment together, it might be more encouraging for both of you to work as partners, sharing both benefits rather than for the other two to work hours.

The next group of corporations, including corporations and limited liability companies, is much more complex. It goes back to early expeditions of the British sea. Rich investors funded ships to search for new resource-rich lands. If the expeditions went well, the ships returned in gold, spices, or slaves. But, if the expeditions went slightly, the ships lost their hands on the sea and drowned. Investors never embarked themselves on these journeys but instead hired crews. The crew was compensated when the vessels returned safely, with the investors cutting their profits, but when the ships sank, the investors did not want to be sued by the families of the crew for losing their families. Thus, companies with limited liability were born. Investors could purchase and sell their shares; although technically their profit potential was limitless, their responsibility for losses was limited to only the amount of their investment. The firm could mismanage its ships, property, and other properties or could sue families of lost crews and be obliged to divide all its properties, but in no case would investors be more than the sum they had already spent on the hook. The limited liability corporation has been viewed as a different company, a false individual, from investors. Indeed, that's the essence of the corporation.

The most important point to consider about this group of companies is that they are all divided from their owners, both legally and financially. This class isolates its owners from the financial and legal responsibilities of the company. If the corporation owes more than it receives, the owners are not directly responsible. If the company harms or damages property, the owners are not directly responsible. But there's one warning: just setting up one of those business organizations does not guarantee this protection; you are responsible for maintaining "corporate formalities." If the plaintiff can, for example, show that you regularly bring in your own business money, pay for certain business expenses directly, or make the business pay for certain personal expenses, they will be able to support you. You must keep the documents properly, conduct proper financial accounting, use corporate funds to pay the corporate debt and hold and officially document annual meetings of shareholders and committees, even though you are the sole shareholder and board member.

In addition to the extra effort, a corporate veil costs something more to create than to shape a non-corporate corporation. You will need a lawyer, and you may even want an accountant. In reality, first, talk to them about which form of company is most suitable. The business may have a different name from the owner(s) and a different TIN or EIN. You may receive some kind of filing receipt from the division of your State Company, it could be called "Corporate articles" or "Organizational articles", and this is a document you will use to open bank accounts under the name of a non-corporate entity instead of a DBA certificated.

The profits of a company are not simply the profits of its owner; you have options about how to deal with them. This is one of the other major benefits of establishing a company: better control over the finances of the business. For a single holding, once spending has been excluded, the remaining benefit is taxable as self-employment, and you will have to pay it yourself, provided that taxes, social insurance, or Medicare were not excluded. For a corporation, the directors and officials (i.e., you) decide how to manage the profits of the company. You may pay it as salaries to managers and other workers (and be liable for the income taxes associated with it), reinvest it in expanding the company, or allocate the benefit to the shareholders (which contributes to lower tax obligations). There are three of them: C (also called "C Corp"), S (or "S Corp"), and the Limited Liability Corporation (LLC).

The conventional business is the C business. The major corporations that you know about are mainly C corps: Proctor & Gamble, Coca Cola, IBM, Frito Lay, Microsoft, and McDonald's. C corps may have an infinite number of shareholders, who may be citizens, foreigners, or other businesses. A small number of shares may hold closely or be traded publicly, such as on the New York Stock Exchange. C businesses have large recordkeeping and financial responsibilities, and as each is viewed as a fake, they pay taxes on their own profits. Some companies like Microsoft don't pay any dividends and reinvest all their earnings efficiently, but most small corporation's shareholders tend to collect their benefit cuts and pay income tax on their distributions. This results in double taxation when the corporation pays the corporate tax on the profit it receives, and then, when it is allocated to it, the owners again pay income tax on that profit.

You may choose to form one of the other companies in order to tackle this double taxation. Who may be an owner of an S corporation has certain limitations, but if the company qualifies, the benefit of the corporation is passed to and is only taxed on its shareholder tax returns once. To form an S corporation, you start by forming a standard C corporation, then submit an application for S care to the IRS and your state tax office. S businesses have long been around and have been prosecuted enough to establish a strong legal precedent. If you don't know the definition, the US legal system mainly functions on a precedent. Instead of endlessly re-inventing the wheel, if you have been on the court for material-like situations, the council will invoke the prior case, and the judge will undoubtedly make a decision equal to that of the preceding judge.

This is one of the key differences with a Limited Liability Company (LLC)-a comparatively young business organization, and no legal precedent for it has been established. So far, I have been told that judges seem to give it the same respect as S businesses, but without such a wide body of authority, there can be no judge to make an unwelcome, uncomfortable decision that would be a precedent for other judges themselves to adopt. Two further distinctions are that an LLC must have an operating agreement and must meet publishing criteria. The business agreement is a basic document that you can build for yourself that outlines certain essential details about the organization and its relationship with its members. Online check for samples or purchase a prototype from a legal aid company or legal form. Publication standards vary according to municipalities, but if you've ever wondered about all these legal notices in your classified newspaper column, people will make these announcements. In New York, LLCs must take such advertisements in a single day on and a weekly publication, each accepted by the local County Clerk, and then send copies of both affidavits of newspaper publications with a form and fee to the Department of State.

Insider Tips to Increase Your Number of Real Estate Investments

So far, it seems as if this year is already a busy year of new prospects. In the real estate investment world, we saw some good opportunities (including tax advantages in the GO zone) last year, and there is a continuous shift in the world of financing for investors. One common topic of some of the real estate investors I was acquainted with was that, while there were additional real estate opportunities in which they wanted to invest, they chose to offer the opportunity because they were financially and in terms of credit.

Although my comments below are not rocket science, I figured we might start jumping before we roll around in the middle of the year. If you want to be increasing the amount of investments in your portfolio and don't wish to offer real estate opportunities that you would usually jump on at heart if you weren't tipped off, then form a partnership!

SO, WHAT IS A PARTNERSHIP?

You can search on the internet and find several definitions of a relationship for those of you who want the info. For the purposes of this section, a partnership is simply a collaboration between two or more organizations that work for mutual benefits. Quick and to the point! That's it. The key I want to stress is that a relationship is beneficial to all interested parties. It has to make "business sense" for those concerned, as I like to say.

APPLYING PARTNERSHIPS TO REAL ESTATE INVESTING

Many real estate investors have the time and experience to both discover and analyze potential opportunities. After a while, however, they lack loans and funds to take action and continue to add to their real estate portfolios. Or investors may have the capital and have little time or experience to determine opportunities. Normally, one of the above (i.e., time, expertise, or money/credit) is generally missing and needs a relationship to be created. Or in other words, you could be an excellent partner if you have one of those things!

MAKING IT ALL WORK TOGETHER

Have you ever heard the saying, "Don't deal with friends"? Some of the best working relationships in real estate investment, as with most companies, are between similar people with the same intentions and visions (but not generally with the same characteristics-see below). If it is not properly handled, a company with friends will dismantle friendship. All I mean is that you should carefully select your business partners. There's nothing worth losing good friends, but nothing rips friends apart like a company that's gone sour.

Choosing your partners is key to a good relationship. Although all partnership elements must be in place (e.g., expertise, time, and money/capital), the synergies between the partners must be focused on their respective functions and responsibilities in the partnership.

For instance, if you are the person who has the expertise to look for a money partner, you probably want to find someone who knows about real estate investments but doesn't really want to do all the research and analysis yourself. That would eventually double the effort and would not be the best use of the partnership's money. Look for complementary features that match the already existing features (or that match your own characteristics). Irrespective of the missing part, you seek someone who is truthful, reasonable, and well-informed.

FORMALIZING THE RELATIONSHIP

There are several ways a relationship can be formed using the above definition. The exact details can vary, depending on the way you walk. Because this is an entrepreneurial relationship, treat it as such and form a legal entity. Please note that several other advantages are not covered here and should be preceded by a lot of posts.

You may, for example, want to create a limited liability company (LLC) covering a specific form of investment (i.e., rental property, land investment, etc.) or a specified locale (i.e., south-west, area of the Mississippi GO Zone) or states (i.e., Florida, Texas, Aribuna, etc.). An LLC consists of sending to the Secretary of State a collection of "Articles of Organization" for the specific state in which you are establishing. Please notice that LLC is not a taxpayer. Profits, losses, etc. move directly through and are recorded on tax returns of the individual member. Most states require that the LLC have an "Operating Arrangement" between the LLC members about its management, etc.

Or, in comparison to an LLC, you might want to establish a true "partnership" or Limited Partnership. There are several different ways of structuring, and all have their own views and reasons for choosing one direction to another. No matter which way you choose, ensure that both involved are in the loop and that they comply with the arrangement, any operating agreements, etc. Furthermore, as the requirements to structure and create a relationship, LLC, etc. differ from state to state, it is best to obtain some professional assistance in establishing your company. As previously mentioned, a properly organized organization has several other advantages.

INCREASE YOUR POTENTIAL

You may see the advantages of collaborations with others with or without a structured arrangement to maximize your real estate potential. Let us assume that you belong to an investment group in real estate and are continuously obtaining quality opportunities. You will then carry out your own due diligence on the project with infinite credit to see if it fits the investment requirements. If it does, everything from the top level will be financed to finance the project and to add it to your portfolio. One day your nice banker and a lending officer will come and say you are taken out; you will not afford any additional projects with your current finances. Besides freeing up capital by selling other assets, a money partner can be found to supply the missing commodity.

You have done more than just add the additional project (which was your first objective) to your portfolio by partnering. Now you have added someone to the immobilization environment and may have built a fantastic board for more projects, companies, etc.

SUMMARY

Immobilien Investing is a genuine team effort. To succeed, you need to work together with elements of time, experience, and capital. Limitations in one of these elements will significantly prevent your investment opportunities in your real estate. You will maximize your total amount of investments by working with others and not miss a great opportunity again.

Incorporation for Home Based Businesses

I'm just a small incorporate; do I really have to integrate it?

Regardless of whether you are a fortune 500 organization employing thousands of workers or an independent company operator, Incorporation is the only way to defend yourself and your personal properties from the threat of litigation. Additional legal benefits of incorporation include:

1. Increased Privacy
2. Reduced Taxes
3. Building Credit
4. Reduced Risk of Audit
5. Enjoying Corporate Benefits
6. Raising Capital

An organization is a legal entity empowered to serve as a scapegoat, decoy, servant, or friend for the good of its shareholders, depending on their needs. You can control an organization without being held accountable for its actions.

If you run a company of any size or consider starting a business, you will have a cost-effective basis for cutting taxable profits, preserving your personal assets, and doing property planning at your best.

1. Tax savings – Correctly organized companies will pay a portion of what anyone in federal taxation would pay for the same personal income, and in some cases, do not pay taxes from the State. The range of tax-saving techniques that can be accomplished by the business structure includes medical care plans, retirement savings, tax contributions, insurance, tourism, entertainment, property, recreational vehicles, and more.

2. Asset Protection-Thousands of cases are filed daily for easy money by individuals, attorneys, and companies. Using a company to protect your personal assets against your company's future liability will provide insurance and peace of mind.

3. Estate Planning-The richest families in America have always understood the benefits of careful property planning. Properly organized within a company, property benefits can be paid without paying property tax. This may mean the

difference between significant wealth for survivors or substantial wealth forced the government to sell the estate just to pay taxes.

What State offers the best benefits for incorporation?

A qualified attorney and accountant can better answer these questions based on the specific circumstances. However, the following details should give you a positive outlook for your discussions.

What is the best structure of the business?

Basically, there are four types of companies C, LLC, Near, and S. Again, please consult a professional business lawyer to determine what is best for your company.

'C' Corporation-the c corporation is a distinct legal entity that can exist or be empowered to defend the shareholder from financial loss for ever. The management of a board of directors and corporate officers is replaced by the owners (shareholders) daily. At shareholder meetings, shareholders elect a Board of Directors.

LLC — Limited Liability Corporation (LLC) otherwise has members rather than shareholders. It may opt to pass on the members of the LLC gains or losses, credits, or deductions. An LLC status eliminates a possible corporate issue of double taxation. Individual representatives can benefit from a taxable income reduction if the business functions at a loss. LLC retains full corporate characteristics, including limited liability, despite its special tax treatment. If you are not sure of what kind of company you should start with, you should choose this one. An LLC can then be transformed into a C business, far easier than transforming a C into an LLC.

Close Company-The Close Company is a statutory act created specifically for small businesses that typically have a small number of shareholders who are related to each other through family relationships, friends, and business partners. Close companies are special cases of regular companies that opt to work in a more casual manner similar to partnerships. Normal companies should hold shareholders and managers' meetings, elect the board of directors, and send written proposals to shareholders on any new corporate action to be voted on at their annual meetings. Family businesses do not typically hold annual meetings since the family takes daily decisions on or around the breakfast table. A Board of Directors is often unnecessary, and so ongoing activities need much less paperwork.

"S" company- S company status shall be given by the IRS to any normal company or close company that meets specific requirements. Domestic companies, with 100 or fewer shareholders of the same class and resident aliens or citizens of the United States, can choose for shareholders to make profits or losses, credits, or deductions in much the same way as partnerships. "S" status prevents the possible corporate issue of "dual taxation;" if the company runs at a loss, individual shareholders can benefit from reduced taxable income. Despite their special tax treatment, S businesses retain complete corporate characteristics, such as limited liability and continuity of existence. If a corporation is a normal "C" corporation or a closer company, for tax purposes, it may become an "S" corporation.

Whatever system you chose and wherever you are, your organization and family will benefit from a carefully designed and implemented corporate strategy. Whatever structure you choose and regardless of where you incorporate, your business and your family will benefit from a carefully planned and executed corporate strategy.

CONCLUSION

The entire premise of investment is that every time the investor spends, they expect their clothing to be returned. The definition of the mutual fund is one most people want to understand, especially the procedures required to allocate their capital gains and dividends.

Most of the time, the problem depends on the organization in which you are associated since it determines when these funds should be allocated. The dividends are extracted from the interest earned from the various securities formed and the portfolio itself. Many trading firms give their investors some dividends, while other firms reinvest this particular amount and then, at a later date, pay a higher dividend.

Mostly when an investor is returned, they think this is too little, but they should be completely inclined towards the rules of the specific contract they have signed, as taxable returns are available. The capital gains stay for more than a year, all these securities must be discussed, and a report must be sent to the investor to prove what happened.

By dealing with these stocks, capital gains are taxable as long-term investments, no matter how long they are acquired. Due to the sharing of the required funds, they are recorded on a special form called 1099-DIV. These procedures are legal and subject to a personal tax duty as an investor on your side.

- How to pay yourself as a SM - **LLC** ?
- We are totally separated from the entity.
- The EIN is the number you use to open a business account. Substitutes to the SSN / SM = single member.

- Member = shareholder.

    LLC ⟼ S Corp (has a lot of rules)
      - forms 2553
      - form 8832

- We give salaries to set employees based on what they think is reasonable.

  - Gross income / Net income.

What we have to deduce from payroll and our salary:

1) Social Security and medicare taxes = 7.65%
2) - QBI deduction = Qualified Business Income deduction. Is 20% deduction on any business income.
3) - Federal and State taxes.
4) - FICA, Fed, State taxes
  . Self - employment tax = 15,3%

1) - Draft OPERATING AGREEMENT - _6 steps_

2) - Apply for E.I.N.

3) - Open a business bank account :
   - Transfer all the funds from your personal account to the business account.
   - You can open a few -

4) - Get business Licenses - ⟶ Real estate

5) - Get [contracts]

6) - Get payroll provider -

Employees : 1099 or W2 -

- Business return
  [Schedule C] ⇒
    Business year strategy :
  = Organizational "expenses"
  = Home office deduction
  = Entity classification erection

  ● Year = [2869.44] for one year :
  ⟶ corporate account - unlimited access to them -

- CLIENT BOOKS
  ↳ own proprietary software.

- Gal CONDON -

Made in the USA
Coppell, TX
18 April 2022